Intervention
for Men
Who Batter

Interpersonal Violence:
The Practice Series
Jon R. Conte, Series Editor

Interpersonal Violence: The Practice Series is devoted to mental health, social service, and allied professionals who confront daily the problem of interpersonal violence. It is hoped that the knowledge, professional experience, and high standards of practice offered by the authors of these volumes may lead to the end of interpersonal violence.

In this series...

Intervention for Men Who Batter

An Ecological Approach

Jeffrey L. Edleson
Richard M. Tolman

Interpersonal Violence:
The Practice Series

SAGE Publications
International Educational and Professional Publisher
Newbury Park   London   New Delhi

For information address:

 SAGE Publications, Inc.
2455 Teller Road
Newbury Park, California 91320
E-mail: order@sagepub.com

SAGE Publications Ltd.
6 Bonhill Street
London EC2A 4PU
United Kingdom

SAGE Publications India Pvt. Ltd.
M-32 Market
Greater Kailash I
New Delhi 110 048 India

Printed in the United States of America

Library of Congress Cataloging-in-Publication Data

Edleson, Jeffrey L.
    Intervention for men who batter : an ecological approach / Jeffrey
L. Edleson, Richard M. Tolman.
        p.   cm.   —(Interpersonal violence: The practice series : 3)
    Includes bibliographical references and index.
    ISBN 0-8039-4264-8.   —ISBN 0-8039-4265-6 (pbk.)
    1. Abusive men—Rehabilitation.   2. Wife abuse—Prevention.
3. Family violence—Prevention.   4. Ecopsychiatry.   I. Tolman,
Richard M.   II. Title.   III. Series.
RC569.5.F3E4   1992
362.82'9286'081—dc20   92-23605
                                                             CIP
96   97   98   99   00   01   11   10   9   8   7   6   5   4

Sage Production Editor: Judith L. Hunter

Contents

This book is dedicated to
Marcie, Daniel, and Eli
Naomi, Arielle, and Emma

Preface

We have both worked with men who batter for more than a decade, in a number of places. Between the two of us, we have worked with batterers in Alaska, New York, Minnesota, Chicago, Israel, and, most recently, Singapore. During this period, we have seen the number and variety of programs explode. We have also read with interest the vast number of articles and books that have recently been published on this topic.

A decade of work and yet we have often felt that the existing programs and literature about programs for men who batter appear fragmented. One person offers a men's group, while another is working in couple counseling, and still others are working with the criminal justice system. We find that many professionals are working separately and with little knowledge of what others are doing or planning. Too often, practitioners go about their work without a comprehensive and integrated understanding of how their work enhances that of the others and can be coordinated with it.

We hope that this book will assist practitioners in the field in standing back from their own work and seeing how their actions both complement and enhance the work of others. We also hope to impart the great wealth of knowledge accumulated during the past 15 years by the thousands of women and men working in this field.

This book is aimed at practitioners and policymakers who seek an overall framework and set of intervention models to draw upon when designing new efforts in their own communities. It presents an integrated, ecological approach to working with men who batter. We attempt to find and emphasize the usefulness of a variety of approaches and the way each approach can be an integral part of a larger whole.

Intervention with violent men is clearly the focus of this book. It is important, however, to stress that battered women are always present in one form or another in the work involved in such efforts. They are also perhaps the more important client when compared with the men. It is, after all, the woman victim who experiences the consequences of successful or unsuccessful intervention with men who batter. Because the consequences of failure may be quite costly to women victims, they have the right to be given regular information about the process and progress of intervention and to have input into its design.

Due to the constraints of space, we have focused this book upon violent men and how to intervene with them in a comprehensive manner. We give attention to the victims throughout but we do not focus on interventions with them. For specific assessment and intervention guidance for working with women and child victims, the reader must look elsewhere.

Chapter 1 provides definitions of woman abuse, the forms it takes, and the effects it has on its victims and their families. The next chapter describes our integrated view of how violence develops, is maintained, and may be ended. Chapter 3 continues with a focus on assessment of abusive men. Chapters 4, 5, and 6 focus on models of intervention. Chapter 4 presents a detailed discussion of small groups as a method for helping men to become nonviolent and respectful of their partner's human rights. Chapter 5 briefly examines individual counseling with men who batter, then focuses on the controversial issues surrounding the use of couple or family counseling with violent men and their victims, and finally provides guidelines for the careful use of such methods. In Chapter 6, we present larger system interventions with a focus on criminal justice systems. In each of the three intervention-oriented chapters, we discuss not only the clinical issues and methods but also what current information exists as to the effectiveness of these types of interventions. In the epilogue, we come back to our integrated approach and argue for additional interventions that have not yet been established.

We acknowledge that this book is very brief and offers only limited information. We consider it an orientation requiring exploration beyond its pages and have included as many up-to-date references as possible to facilitate this process.

Finally, there are many people who deserve recognition for having made possible this book and, more important, its ideas. Our wives, Marcie Stein and Naomi Woloshin, have offered us the chance to understand the pressures and joys of intimate relationships. With them, we have experienced that conflicts as partners and parents, while often difficult and tension filled, can be resolved in nonviolent and mutually rewarding ways.

We must thank the many practitioners and clients of the Domestic Abuse Project in Minneapolis, Minnesota, who have created a truly integrated intervention in woman abuse. We have both greatly benefited from clinical and research experiences at DAP.

In Chicago, the practitioners and clients at the Crisis Center for South Suburbia in Worth, Illinois, and at Sarah's Inn, Oak Park, have contributed invaluably to the development of these ideas and experiences.

While there are many individuals to thank, we would like to single out a few: our colleagues at the Domestic Abuse Project—Mary Pat Brygger, Joanne Kittel, Roger Grusznski, James Brink, Cheryl Howard, Lynn Jacobs, Carol Arthur, Ann Moore, Jack Rusinoff, Joan Bilinkoff, Denise Gamache, and Jean Rambow; also Christine Call, Evelyn Montgomery, Pauline Geary, and Alex Maximiac at Sarah's Inn; Keith Wiger of Anchorage, Alaska; Zvi Eisikovits in Israel; and Esther Tzer Wong in Singapore.

Our employers and colleagues at the University of Minnesota School of Social Work and the University of Illinois Jane Addams College of Social Work have also greatly facilitated this book with years of support. We have both also benefited from the mentoring of Professor Sheldon D. Rose of the University of Wisconsin, who has taught us how to perform field research and to write about it in an accessible way. Sheldon has also offered a wonderful model for integrating a meaningful personal life with the demands of our work.

1

Introduction

In a 1942 essay titled "The Best Field for Ahimsa," Mahatma Gandhi wrote:[1]

> I propose to invite attention today to . . . the best field for the operation of non-violence. This is the family field. . . . Non-violence as between the members of such families should be easy to practise. If that fails, it means that we have not developed the capacity for pure non-violence. For, the love we have to practise towards our relatives or colleagues in our family or institutions, we have to practise towards our foes, dacoits, etc. If we fail in one case, success in the other is a chimera . . . *ahimsa* is best learnt in the domestic school, and I can say from experience that, if we secure success there, we are sure to do so everywhere else. For a non-violent person the whole world is one family. He will thus fear none, nor will others fear him. (p. 299)

This book is about one form of violence in intimate relationships, that of woman battering. It is about the injuries and deaths men's violence creates among their women partners and children as well as the fear and terror this violence engenders. Throughout this book,

1

we consider both physically violent acts and psychological maltreatment. This book, however, is also about the many social efforts now under way to bring about an end to this violence and psychological maltreatment through intervention with men who batter. We offer a comprehensive vision of how society can intervene with violent men to foster intimate relationships where living free of violence is considered a basic human right.

❏ **An Integrated Framework**

The assessment and intervention procedures offered throughout this book are based on an integrated framework for understanding the problem of woman abuse and identifying interventions to stop it. Our integrated framework may best be labeled an "ecological" approach within which we apply a number of other perspectives such as historical, feminist, and social learning analyses as well as an awareness of the impact of ethnicity and class. Our framework, as described in much greater detail in Chapter 2, draws on the strongest aspects of selected existing frameworks and theories in a way that leads to the possibility of multiple, complementary interventions to eliminate woman abuse. We introduce the technical language of the ecological framework and specific theories in Chapter 2 but then try to apply the ideas without the technical jargon in the remaining chapters. We do this to offer the reader a clear outline of our integrated approach in Chapter 2 while enhancing the readability of remaining chapters on assessment and intervention.

❏ **The Forms of Violence**

Woman abuse takes many forms and, as societies come to recognize it as a problem, the terms used to describe such violence and define its scope often expand. The North American public is most aware of physical violence against women, and the definition of physically violent behavior is increasingly refined in the law, through measurement in research, and through community actions. Other forms of violence, such as psychological maltreatment, are not as clearly defined but may be no less damaging to the victims. As we have already stated, throughout this book, we consider both physically violent acts and psychological maltreatment to be important targets of intervention. It is necessary to pause here and consider our definitions of *abuse*, both physical and psychological, on which the remainder of this book focuses.

PHYSICAL VIOLENCE

Perhaps the most widely used definition of physical abuse is one proposed by Straus, Gelles, and Steinmetz (1980) in their landmark national survey of family violence. They defined *violence* as "an act carried out with the intention, or perceived intention, of causing physical pain or injury to another person" (p. 20). Using this definition, violence may vary from a shove to the use of a lethal weapon against another person. Straus and Gelles

> *Violence may vary from a shove to the use of a lethal weapon against another person.*

(1988) later offer the term *severe violence* to indicate a subgroup of violent acts that have a "much greater potential for producing an injury" (p. 16). These include acts such as kicking, punching, choking, threats with a weapon, and the use of a weapon. They point out, however, that to understand violence requires more information than simple descriptions of the acts that occurred. Contextual factors such as what type of injury resulted and the motivation of the perpetrator are important pieces of information. A violent act in one context may be viewed much more seriously than the same act in another context depending on the influence of other factors.

Surveys of randomly selected U.S. couples have found that from 10.8% to 22% of the couples studied reported some type of woman abuse (see Straus & Gelles, 1988). The largest sample available was one surveyed by Straus and Gelles (1986), who found 11.6% of 6,002 households reported physical violence by the man and that in 3.4% of all households the man was perpetrating severe violence against his woman partner. This latter figure translates to an estimate that approximately 1.8 million U.S. women are being severely beaten each year (Straus & Gelles, 1990). Because of the social stigma and danger involved in making reports of violence, most researchers and practitioners agree that these estimates reflect substantial underreporting of violence against women.

The category of severe physical violence also includes rape and other forms of sexual assault. While rape and woman abuse are often thought to be different phenomena, Finkelhor and Yllo (1982) point out that the great majority of rapes are thought to occur between intimate partners or acquaintances. Several studies have found that between 9% and 14% of women report having been forced to perform some type of sex with their intimate male partners (Hanneke, Shields, & McCall, 1986; Russell, 1982).

The FBI has estimated that a rape is reported every 6 minutes in the United States and that these reports represent only 1 in 10 actual incidents (Federal Bureau of Investigation [FBI], 1979, 1986). A survey of 6,159 students at 32 colleges found that 27.5% of the women sampled reported having been a victim of rape or attempted rape at some time since the age of 14. The results also indicated that 8.3% of the women reported a rape or attempted rape during the previous 6 months (Koss, Gidycz, & Wisniewski, 1987).

The most brutal form of physical violence is murder. Mercy and Saltzman (1989) reviewed 10 years of FBI statistics on homicides in the United States and found 16,595 spousal homicides (8.8% of total). The risk of being murdered by a spouse was 1.3 times greater for women than for men. In a study of murders in Britain, approximately 25% of all homicides were committed by current or former intimate partners with the overwhelming majority of victims being women (Edwards, 1985).

Physical and sexual abuse of female children is perhaps another, earlier form of woman abuse. This book does not focus on child abuse. It is worth noting, however, that recent surveys have found that approximately 3 to 4 of every 1,000 children are physically abused each year (Starr, 1988; Straus & Gelles, 1990) and from 0.7 to 1.4 per 1,000 children are sexually abused yearly (Wolfe, Wolfe, & Best, 1988). The great majority of sexual abuse reports are of girls abused by men (Wolfe et al., 1988).

Rampant violence in intimate relationships has created a situation where the American home is now considered the most likely place that a woman will be beaten, raped, or murdered. In this context, many women also speak of the power other forms of abuse, such as psychological maltreatment, acquire.

PSYCHOLOGICAL MALTREATMENT

Broadly construed, psychological maltreatment may be considered any behavior that is harmful to the well-being of a spouse. Physical violence and the concomitant use of other psychologically abusive behaviors, such as verbal intimidation, isolation, and financial manipulation, are viewed as creating a power imbalance that enhances a man's ability to dominate his partner (Tolman & Edleson, 1989).

Given that some emotional pain and lack of cooperation characterizes most human relationships, a definition of psychological maltreatment that includes any kind of harmful behavior would fail to distinguish severe, seriously harmful cases of such maltreatment. Social intervention requires that we be able to clearly define the occurrence of psychological maltreatment in a manner that will allow us to identify a pattern of maltreatment in which the man is harming his partner. The small literature on psychological maltreatment suggests that it may be useful to use a continuum to define it (Garbarino, Guttmann, & Seeley, 1986). On one end are isolated hurtful behaviors that may occur in most relationships, such as withdrawing momentarily or speaking sharply in anger. On the other end of the continuum is pervasive, one-sided, severe psychological torture paralleling intentional brainwashing and mistreatment of prisoners of war (Graham, Rawlings, & Rimini, 1988). It is the men who subject women to maltreatment on the severe end of this continuum who are the most difficult yet often the most important targets of intervention.

Psychological maltreatment almost always accompanies physical maltreatment. A strict separation of psychological from physical maltreatment may be illusory, as physical abuse may often have aspects of psychological maltreatment. For example, in addition to the physical pain and intimidation a woman may feel when her husband slaps her in front of her child or other family members, she may also feel humiliated, embarrassed, and demeaned. Some women report that these latter feelings may even be the more harmful and debilitating effects of their partners' physically abusive behavior.

In trying to categorize psychological maltreatment, it becomes clear that a behavior may have more than one type of impact and that there is a great deal of overlap and interconnection between different types of psychological maltreatment. For example, a verbal putdown in front of others could fall into several categories. Most obviously, it is degrading to be insulted in front of other people. The same behavior may contribute to isolation because a victim of such verbal abuse may want to avoid social situations in which this type of abuse may recur. A putdown may create fear, because it signals a possibility that physical abuse may follow. A putdown may also be a technique for enforcing a demand made by the abuser.

In another essay (see Tolman, 1992), we have proposed that psychological maltreatment may be divided into 9 categories: (a) creation of fear through various types of threats; (b) isolation of partner by limiting or prohibiting her contact with others; (c) monopolization of her life by constantly monitoring her or interfering with her social or work life; (d) economic abuse by limiting her access to family financial resources and decisions or by misusing family funds; (e) degradation of partner by forcing her to perform humiliating acts or by verbally humiliating her; (f) rigid sex role expectations and trivial requests based on them that humiliate her; (g) psychological destabilization that purposefully creates doubt in the victim about the validity of her perceptions; (h) emotional and interpersonal withholding, sometimes for long periods of time without explanation; and (i) contingent expressions of love that require compliance with the abuser's demands. Similarly, Pence (1989) has developed a model of woman abuse that presents a series of 8 psychologically abusive behaviors in the form of a wheel encircled by various forms of physical violence and with power and control at the center. Clearly, the clinical utility of the categories of psychological abuse in Pence's model or those listed here must not be judged by their precision or exclusivity but by their ability to provide guidance in assessing and understanding the presence of psychological maltreatment in a relationship.

To date, there are few data on the degree to which any of these categories of psychological maltreatment occur in relationships where men are also using physical violence. Treatment evaluations that have measured threats of physical violence have found them more difficult to eliminate than physical violence (see Edleson & Grusznski, 1988; Edleson & Syers, 1990; Tolman, Beeman, & Mendoza, 1987). Most testimonies by battered women also relay descriptions of relationships where severe psychological maltreatment occurs frequently and is only punctuated by acts of physical violence (Pagelow, 1981).

EFFECTS OF ABUSE

It is not surprising that, as a result of physical violence and psychological maltreatment, women and children experience serious difficulties. The effects of abuse take the form of both increased physical illness and emotional problems among women and child victims. They also take an economic toll on individuals and on society.

Women victims of severe violence have been found to be 3 times more likely to be in poor health than women who have experienced no violence. The same study found that victims of severe violence spend twice as much time in bed due to illness and experience stress-related problems more often than women who live in violence-free environments (Straus & Gelles, 1987). Another study reported that 30% of all women admitted to an emergency room in a large university hospital stated that their injuries were the result of battering (McLeer & Anwar, 1989). In this same study, the younger the woman, the more likely her injuries resulted from a beating, with 42% of the 18- to 20-year-olds identifying their injuries as resulting from abuse.

Emotional effects on women may be more devastating than the physical ones. Gelles and Harrop (1989), using national survey data on 3,002 women, reported that, among women not being physically abused, only 3 in 1,000 thought about taking their own lives "fairly often" or "very often" during the year surveyed. This contrasted sharply with 46 severely abused women in every 1,000 who contemplated suicide as frequently. With few exceptions, Gelles and Harrop (1989) found that "the higher the level of violence experienced, the greater the proportion of women reporting a form of psychological distress" (p. 407). Additional empirical evidence confirms the degree of harm caused by psychological maltreatment. Tolman and Bhosley (1991) interviewed women one year after their male partners had been involved in group treatment for battering and found that psychological maltreatment was a powerful predictor of the woman's psychosocial problems, whether or not the men had again been violent toward their partners. Straus, Sweet, and Vissing (1989) report preliminary findings from a general population survey indicating that, regardless of the presence of physical abuse, the more verbal aggression a woman receives from her spouse, the greater the probability that she will be depressed.

Women are not the only ones who are affected by the violence directed toward them. The couple's children have been called the "forgotten" or "unintended" victims (Elbow, 1982; Rosenbaum & O'Leary, 1981a). They, too, may suffer from either direct abuse or witnessing the abuse of their mother. Several recent reviews of the literature (see Fantuzzo & Lindquist, 1989; Jaffe, Wolfe, & Wilson, 1990) have outlined the possible impact that observing violence may have on a child's development. Their findings indicated that children who witness family violence may experience lower levels of social competency, lower academic achievement, and a variety of emotional problems including depression, suicidal behavior, and insomnia. Little is known and better studies are certainly required to determine how some children develop more serious difficulties than others and how a large number of children develop successful coping strategies.

Society also bears an economic burden resulting from woman abuse. Using 1980 data on 192,000 assaults within families, the National Crime Survey (Bureau of Justice Statistics, 1980) reported that these assaults resulted in 175,500 days of lost work, 99,800 days of hospitalization, and total annual health care costs of more than $44.3 million. Straus (1986) estimated that battered women require more than 1.4 million medical visits each year to care for injuries their partners have inflicted. Researchers have yet to quantify the wide array of health, education, and criminal justice resources devoted to this problem.

These data on social costs and on the incidence of both physical violence and psychological maltreatment show this problem to be so pervasive that one might question explanatory models that do not encompass social-structural factors. The staggering impact of this problem on individuals, families, social institutions, and the society as a whole requires an integrated framework, such as outlined in the next chapter, for understanding and intervening.

❏ An Overview of the Book

This book provides an overview of varied interventions with men who batter that aim to end the types of abuse described above. It is aimed at practitioners and policymakers who seek an overall framework and set of intervention models to draw upon when designing new efforts in their own communities.

Intervention with violent men is the focus of this book. As we stated in the preface, battered women and their children must be considered when intervening with men who batter. This book will not, however, offer specific guidance for working with women and child victims.

Women and children are often the first to experience the effects of successful intervention. Sadly, they are also the first to feel the results of failed efforts. Because the consequences of failure may be quite costly to women and child victims, victims have the right to be regularly informed about the process and progress of intervention as well as contribute to its design. Interventions with men who batter must also be accountable to programs working on behalf of battered women and to those policy makers and funders who direct scarce resources toward the support of these efforts. Such accountability requires that intervenors carefully measure the effects of their own work and widely disseminate their findings. To reinforce this notion of accountability, we conclude each chapter by presenting a model of intervention with a review of the current findings regarding that particular approach.

We start in the next chapter by defining important terms and describing our integrated view of how violence develops, is maintained, and may be ended. Chapter 3 continues with a focus on assessment of abusive men. Chapter 4, 5, and 6 focus on models of intervention. Chapter 4 presents a detailed discussion of small groups as a method for helping men to become nonviolent and respectful of their partner's human rights. Chapter 5 briefly examines individual counseling with men who batter, then focuses on the controversial issues surrounding the use of couple or family counseling with violent men and their victims, and finally provides guidelines for the careful use of such methods. In Chapter 6, we present larger system interventions with a focus on criminal justice systems. In each of the three intervention-oriented chapters, we discuss not only the clinical issues and methods but also what current information exists as to the effectiveness of these types of interventions. In the epilogue, we come back to our integrated approach and argue for additional interventions that have not yet been established.

❏ Note

1. *Ahimsa* is the practice of nonviolence.

2

A Comprehensive
Ecological Approach

This book is based on an integrated framework for understanding the problem of woman abuse and identifying interventions to stop it. As we have stated, our framework draws on the strongest aspects of selected existing frameworks and theories and leads to the possibility of multiple, complementary interventions to eliminate woman abuse. The framework may best be labeled an "ecological" approach within which we apply a number of other perspectives such as historical, feminist, and social learning analyses as well as an awareness of the impact of ethnicity and class.

❏ The Ecological Framework

Social problems and particularly woman abuse require a framework for understanding and intervening that takes into account the complexity of such phenomena and offers a variety of points at which intervention may be attempted. It is within a complex social ecology that violence is initiated and maintained. It is also within this ecology that intervention occurs. Thus a comprehensive ecological framework that identifies *multiple* systems in interaction offers a potentially powerful tool for both assessment and design of interventions.

The most visible proponent of an ecological approach to human development and problems is Bronfenbrenner (1977, 1979, 1986). Others (e.g., Carlson, 1984; Dutton, 1985) have taken this framework and applied it to the specific phenomenon of woman abuse. From the ecological view, a series of systems interact in a web of relationships that affect the development and maintenance of violent behaviors. At the center of the ecological model used here are the individual violent man and his battered partner, who engage in ever changing interactions directly and indirectly with or in four systems: micro, meso, exo, and macro. The individual interacts in and is influenced by these different systems, which, in turn, interact with each other.

MICROSYSTEM

The microsystem includes those interactions in a particular setting in which a person directly engages as well as the subjective meanings assigned to them. For the violent man and battered woman, an important microsystem is that of the family. Others include work environments, the neighborhood, church, and social clubs or sports teams in which they participate. While microsystems include a direct set of interactions and the meanings attached to them in one setting, the combined network of interrelationships among the variety of important microsystems in which one person participates is labeled the mesosystem.

MESOSYSTEM

The mesosystem is often overlooked in the analysis of woman abuse. The mesosystem includes the linkages between microsystems in a person's social environment. Linkages may include those between nuclear family and the place of work, the children's school, an extended family, or a network of peers. The mesosystem also includes linkages with social institutions such as the police, courts, and social services. When a family is particularly isolated or secretive, the possibility of an effective response originating in the mesosystem may be limited in that there are few interactions with others. What linkages do exist may give conflicting messages. For example, some relatives may reinforce the man's use of violence "to keep her in line," while police ignore it, and battered women's advocates are actively opposing the man's violence.

The mesosystem is often the focus of many contemporary community-based approaches to intervening in woman abuse, some of which will be described in Chapter 6. Coordinating various microsystems in a family's ecology into a mesosystem providing a consistent message that violence is not to be permitted is often the goal of intervention. The story of one violent man is a good example of the power of the mesosystem. His wife had called the police for the first time in 20 years of being abused by him. After being arrested and later released, he told a coworker that his wife and the police "screwed" him. The coworker, himself in a treatment group for woman abuse, confronted him and told him he needed to take responsibility for his behavior. In the same day's paper, the man read an article about a coordinated community effort to intervene in woman abuse. When talking to a social worker, he recalled that the article "said that the courts and police and social workers were all getting together to stop abuse. You know what, it's going to work," he added.

EXOSYSTEM

Relationships that indirectly affect the individual violent man are the focus of the exosystem and the macrosystem. The exosystem includes those interactions in which others engage that have some type of eventual impact on the man's behavior and thinking. For example, the criminal justice coordination efforts the man read about in his newspaper would represent his exosystem. Police, prosecutors, judges, probation officers, social workers, and battered women's advocates who meet together to map a strategy for consistently responding to perpetrators of violence form a separate micro-system that indirectly, through the professionals' subsequent imple-mentation of policies, influences his environment. The exosystem is then the combination of microsystems in which others participate but in which the man does not participate directly.

MACROSYSTEM

Even more indirect but still very important to the individual vio-lent man and successful intervention with him is the macrosystem. The macrosystem is, as Bronfenbrenner (1979) terms it, the "set of blueprints" at a cultural, ethnic group, or social class level that dic-tate certain consistencies among similar settings. For example, fam-ily structures among middle-class families in the United States exhibit remarkable similarity. This becomes even more evident when such family structures are contrasted with those of tribal families in the highlands of New Guinea or of low-caste families in rural India. Family organization in each of these cultures most often conforms to the "blueprints" of the particular macrosystem in which they exist. In the same sense, American values concerning the "ideal" husband or wife may differ significantly from those of other cul-tures. These overarching rules of organization within a society have an immense impact on the way in which individuals interact at all levels of the ecology. The effect of macrosystemic beliefs is particu-larly visible when one listens to violent men talk about what "a hus-band is supposed" to be and how "a wife is supposed" to act.

CHRONOSYSTEM

The individual violent man brings a personal history of develop-ment to bear on his interactions in microsystems. In the same sense, societies, ethnic groups, and classes bring group histories to bear on their current macrosystemic beliefs and interpersonal blueprints. To ignore this fact would be to deny the importance of collective and individual history in our everyday interactions. From our perspec-tive, one problem with the ecological framework has been the absence of history as a system that affects all other contemporary systems. In a more recent work, Bronfenbrenner (1986) has partially resolved this problem by labeling personal historical experience as the "chronosystem." Similarly, Dutton (1985, 1988) has labeled this individual historical experience and the beliefs based upon it as the "ontogenetic system." Bronfenbrenner's and Dutton's use of these terms, however, is focused on the individual, his or her personal development, and the immediate environments he or she experiences.

In light of the importance we and others attach to historical antecedents to current social attitudes about and interventions in woman abuse, the chronosystem should be extended to include the histories of all systems in the ecology including the long developmental history of cultural attitudes and actions regarding male-female relationships. To differentiate individual from group historical development would fragment the ecological approach. We will therefore use the chronosystem to denote the spectrum of historical factors ranging from a man's personal developmental history and the current beliefs based upon it to the history underlying all other ecological systems. We assume that the broadly defined chronosystem may significantly influence how various other systems interact with each other on a day-to-day basis. The chronosystem also provides greater depth to the ecological framework and may allow for an analysis of how system interactions change over time.

The ecological framework applied here then includes the violent man, with his particular history, in direct interactions with others in varied settings that form a multitude of microsystems. This collection of microsystems forms the man's mesosystem. Others in the man's microsystem engage in relationships within other settings where the man is not directly involved, forming exosystems in this man's ecology. Still more indirect are the cultural, ethnic group, and class rules that form his macrosystem. And, finally, there is the chronosystem, which reflects the depth of time and its effect on all the contemporary systems at play.

❏ Underlying Assumptions

Basic to our framework are the assumptions that living free of violence is a human right that should be enjoyed equally by all and that an individual is personally responsible for his or her behavior toward others.

VIOLENCE-FREE ENVIRONMENTS AS A HUMAN RIGHT

We propose that in contemporary society all individuals, regardless of gender or other distinguishing factors, are entitled to make life choices without being inhibited by physical violence and psychological maltreatment. This right has been particularly difficult for women around the world to achieve.

The right to make choices on an equal basis with men and without the fear of reprisals has been reinforced by a growing set of international accords on human rights as well as continuing changes in American views of intimate relationships between men and women. In December 1979, the U.N. General Assembly adopted the *Convention on the Elimination of All Forms of Discrimination Against Women* (United Nations, 1979). The *Convention* includes 16 articles that define basic rights for women. Many of these articles describe as rights the very behaviors that both physical violence and psychological maltreatment often aim to curb. For example, the *Convention* includes the rights to free movement (Article 15), to work and to the free choice of employment (Article 11), and to equality in the management of family resources (Article 16). In addition, it requires governments to embed the principle of equality in national constitutions, legal codes, or other laws and to ensure that such equality is implemented (Article 2). By 1990, more than 100 nations had ratified it; however, the United States has yet to do so.

In addition to the *Convention*, a number of U.N. conferences have, in recent years, passed several resolutions on family violence and issued reports such as one by the 1986 Expert Group Meeting on Violence in the Family that focused special attention on woman abuse (United Nations, 1987). These actions have, during the past decade, clearly raised equality of treatment for women to the level of a human right and identified woman abuse as a major violation of this right.

We believe that the views of the U.S. public are changing so that both physical and psychological maltreatment of a woman by her intimate partner are increasingly perceived as antisocial behavior that violates her basic rights as a human being. Our framework assumes this right to live free of both physical violence and psychological maltreatment.

PERSONAL CHOICE AND RESPONSIBILITY

Another assumption we make is that each individual is responsible for his or her own behavior toward others. Certainly, as will be seen throughout this book, we see as very important the multiple social factors outside the individual that encourage certain behaviors while inhibiting others. Yet we also recognize that in any social environment there are many competing and conflicting influences. In fact, a major part of our integrated framework rests on the assumption that such influences can be altered through intervention.

This assumption is consistent with Skinner's (1974) view of control and countercontrol. Social learning theory recognizes that, while personal freedom is limited by genetic and environmental constraints, individuals still maintain an ability to *counter* these influences by developing new alternatives. From a very different perspective, existential writers have also recognized that even in environments such as Nazi concentration camps there are still individual choices in daily life (see Frankl, 1959).

The alternative behaviors from which violent men may choose are much less constrained than those considered by either Skinner or Frankl. The influences of various ecological factors are great but, in the final analysis, we assume that certain choices are available to the individual. A man selects from among possible alternative responses available to him when he is confronted with a difficult situation. The use of violent or psychologically abusive behaviors in a particular situation involves a choice to use them over other, nonviolent and more respectful behaviors.

❑ The Historical Context of Woman Abuse

Also underlying current interactions are, as we pointed out earlier, historical events or those based in the chronosystem. For example, popular beliefs about woman abuse that are rooted in history are part of the ecology in which violence takes root and is maintained. Thus an important factor in understanding both the sources of violence and how to intervene in them may be the historical foundation on which our current understandings of this problem are built.

The little information available concerning the history of woman abuse is almost exclusively based upon European and U.S. cultures. Most feminist historical reviews reach back to the Roman Empire and then quickly move to examples from Judeo-Christian writings and thought throughout the centuries (see Davidson, 1977; Dobash & Dobash, 1979; Spitzer, 1985). It is clear from these reviews that, for most of recorded Western history, women have been viewed as men's property at worst or as the subjects of their rule at best.

Evolving popular beliefs often lead to modifications in the way a profession, ethnic group, or society thinks about itself and the options it considers when making changes. This occurs regularly in scientific fields (see Kuhn, 1962; Mahoney, 1976), and changes around the world offer examples of how widespread revisions in popular thinking about one's own history may influence how certain problems are perceived and what solutions might be considered acceptable. The past 150 years have witnessed such a change regarding woman abuse. Violence against women has been increasingly recognized as a *social problem* and, at least in some societies, efforts to change how the rights of husbands and wives are defined and how social institutions respond to incidents of woman abuse have been initiated (see Bauer & Ritt, 1983; Edleson, 1991a, 1991b; L. Gordon, 1988; Pleck, 1987).

The revision of historical understandings of woman abuse occurred in the context of a reinvigorated women's rights movement in the late 1960s and throughout the 1970s. These revisions must be considered an important "systems change" that helped lay the groundwork for the immense changes that have occurred during the past 15 years in U.S. society's response to woman abuse. As history has progressed, the way in which society views men's violence against fellow family members has changed. What was once defined as the basic right of a husband to "chastise" his wife (see Dobash & Dobash, 1979) is now often labeled as antisocial behavior that violates the rights of the women and child victims. This has led some to more closely examine the differences in power between men and women.

❏ Power and Gender in Relationships

The issue of power in families has been the focus of at least three decades of study (see McDonald, 1980; Safilios-Rothschild, 1970). In general, *power* has been defined as the ability of one partner to potentially or actually modify the behavior of the other when a conflict exists (Rollins & Bahr, 1976). Similarly, *power* has been defined as the ability of one person to gain disproportionate access to resources that determine the direction of the lives of the people in the relationship or family (Bograd, 1988). Gillespie (1971) has pointed out that macrosystemic factors have traditionally placed obstacles in the way of women gaining equal power with men in intimate relationships.

The concept of power, its differential distribution in U.S. society by gender, and its use in controlling others is central to feminist views of violence against women. An ecological examination of power and how it is distributed differently among men and women leads to an investigation of interactions between the family and other systems in the ecology. This view of abuse is one commonly held by a wide spectrum of practitioners in the area. It has been formally incorporated into many batterers' treatment programs.

Power as a factor in relationships has often been minimized or ignored when ecological frameworks have been applied in interventions with violent men and battered women. Instead of examining one partner's power over another, many family therapists have focused on reciprocal transactions between two systems (man and woman). One example of this view is expressed by Lane and Russell (1989), who state: "In the purist sense, we view violence in couples as communication about their relationship. Violent behavior is a dangerous and powerful message that frequently occurs as a crescendo in the couples' symmetrical dance" (p. 144).

The view that violence is part of a reciprocal dance focuses only on the micro interaction between the violent man and the battered woman. Others have acknowledged the issue of power in relation-ships but argued that "conjugal" violence is not an issue of gender but one solely of power and control. The overwhelming evidence, however, points to gender as a central force that cannot be ignored when examining the use of coercive power in American society. Ignoring long-standing historical and cultural biases that favor men may even act to enhance long-standing social biases against women (Bograd, 1984). We see such views of power-absent or gender-absent interactions as flawed because they minimize or ignore factors that have long developed in the chronosystem and are expressed in all other contemporary systems. We view this microsystemic myopia as "context stripping" (Bronfenbrenner, 1979) that examines only part of the picture while ignoring the entire canvas. In other words, ig-noring the historical and cultural power imbalances between men and women in intimate relationships and in society at large strips these interactions of what we believe are critically important factors that play themselves out in daily life.

One need only examine daily American life to see how embedded gender differences have become. Men as a class earn higher in-comes, their work is more likely to be given a higher status than that of women, financial credit is extended to them more readily, cultural expectations lead men to couple with women who are usually shorter and physically smaller, and the police and courts have generally ignored men's use of violence against their intimate partners.

Some men gain power by coercing others through the use of vio-lence or threats of it. Power is gained more often, however, by men making the most decisions or more important decisions in a rela-tionship, by controlling the flow of financial or material resources to intimate partners, and by controlling, with the threat of sanctions, both his partner's social interactions with others and his sexual relations with her. Bograd (1988) and others point out that even men who do not use violence against women also benefit by the way all women are forced to curtail their life activities for fear that they may be subjected to violence.

Men's differential use of power is reinforced through consistent macrosystem messages condoning the use of coercive power tactics. At the same time, women are also given clear messages about their behavior. They are called "aggressive" when the same behavior by men would be termed "assertive." They are called "loose" or "easy" when a man engaging in the same behavior is termed a "Don Juan" or "woman's man." These historical and cultural influences are played out in daily events by the messages community institutions such as police, schools, and hospitals give to individual men, women, and children.

❏ Ethnicity and Class

While gender may be an important factor in determining power within relationships, neither ethnicity nor class should be overlooked. Not only do ethnicity and class influence power within relationships, they also play an important role in how society responds to violent men and their victims. As we will discuss later in this book, a black or Hispanic man is likely to be treated more harshly by the criminal justice system than will his white counterpart. Part of this is the result of racial and ethnic biases that permeate our society. It may also be partially the result of class differences in the resources a man brings to his defense. That is, white American men are more likely to have the financial resources to hire a private defense attorney than are minority men due to the historical effects of racism and the relatively lower class status of most minorities in the United States.

Drawing on Gordon's (1964) work, Devore and Schlesinger (1987) have used the term *ethclass* to denote the combined role that social class and ethnicity play in defining the basic conditions of one's life. An individual's ethclass is the intersection between his or her ethnic group and social class memberships. Thus a poor black man is likely to be treated differently by social systems than either a middle-class black man or a poor white man.

We see the combined effects of ethnicity and class as important factors in both understanding the sources of men's violent behavior and in the design of societal intervention to end such behavior. Understanding chronosystemic aspects of racism and class hierarchy and how such historical factors influence responses of contemporary systems provides often critical information about how an individual man is behaving toward his partner, how actors from various systems are responding to him, and how he and others in his ethnic group or class will view certain types of intervention.

The design of interventions should be "ethnic sensitive" (see Devore & Schlesinger, 1987; Lum, 1986; Pinderhughes, 1989). That is, interventions are likely to be more effective if they incorporate explicit design elements that take account of the ethnic group histories as well as the classes of a particular community. We should add, however, that, while cultural and class traditions should be explicitly addressed, we do not subscribe to "cultural relativism" to the degree that we would accept violence as an appropriate response in one culture but not in another. In this sense, we are absolutists in that we view violent and psychologically abusive behavior as inappropriate in any context unless it is used temporarily for self-defense.

❑ Social Learning

The use of violence to gain power is not an irrational, unintentional, or impulsive act. In most cases, we see violence as an intentional behavior that serves to systematically enhance a perpetrator's coercive control over others in his world. Thus violence may be viewed as a behavior that serves a power-enhancing *function* for the perpetrator.

From a social learning perspective, the successful use of violence will increase the likelihood that it will be used again.

From a social learning perspective, the successful use of violence will increase the likelihood that it will be used again. Any behavior that achieves a visible goal—whether compliance with a man's wishes or social approval from his peers for the way he treats his wife—is likely to be repeated when similar circumstances present themselves (Bandura, 1973, 1977; Gambrill, 1977).

The conditions of a situation that make violence possible or impossible are termed *antecedents* and the benefits gained or costs incurred through the use of coercive power are termed *contingent consequences* (see Gambrill, 1977). Antecedents can be extremely varied. While often erroneously attributed only to microsystem interaction, antecedents may include all of those factors in the chronosystem that precede the particular event (see Hamberger & Lohr, 1989; Kunkel, 1975; Nietzel, Winett, MacDonald, & Davidson, 1977). Thus a man's experience that neighbors, family members, and the police will not intervene in domestic disputes may set the stage for the use of violence without sanction. Similarly, the macrosystemic messages about what it is to be a "real man" or a "supportive wife" are also antecedent conditions that may enhance the likelihood of certain actions taking place in a particular family. In the same sense, a man's peer group that reinforces his "keeping his woman in line" may also enhance the likelihood of future violent and abusive behavior. Finally, as Bandura (1973, 1977) and his colleagues have found, one of the most important forms of social learning is *modeling*. That is, people learn by viewing the antecedents, behavior, and consequences that occur (or are modeled) in others' lives. If we see others gaining from the use of violent behavior, we are more likely to use that behavior ourselves.

Antecedents and contingent consequences also work to inhibit violent behavior. If the mesosystem, consisting of a variety of microsystems such as police, courts, and community activists, now acts in concert and creates a consistent message that severe sanctions will be applied in cases of violence, the consistent use of sanctions (contingent consequences) may decrease the likelihood of a man using violence in the future. Seeing that the police are arresting other men (modeling) will also change the antecedent conditions under which a man would judge violence a feasible alternative (see Carmody & Williams, 1987).

Social learning theory and resulting cognitive-behavioral treatment procedures offer guides for taking the more abstract concepts of the ecological framework and feminist analysis to an operational or practice level. Cognitive-behavioral procedures offer direction in analyzing functional relationships between violent behavior and the events that both precede and follow it. Performing such analyses often enhances our ability to see points of possible intervention (Edleson, 1984a). Once focused on an intervention point, it is possible to draw upon a variety of empirically supported intervention procedures derived from social learning theory. Cognitive-behavioral procedures are widely used with batterers in small groups (Saunders, 1989; Tolman & Edleson, 1989; Tolman & Saunders, 1988) and with couples (Margolin, 1979; Rosenbaum & O'Leary, 1986) but have seldom been explicitly applied in larger system interventions.

❑ An Integrated Approach

We have put forth an approach to woman abuse that rests on the foundation of an ecological framework and is informed by historical, feminist, and social learning concepts with attention to issues of ethnicity and class. The integration of these perspectives, despite some contradictions between them, creates a model that has strong explanatory power as well as offering practical guidance.

We are certainly not the first authors to have proposed the integration of various aspects of these perspectives. Ganley (1989) has recently offered a cohesive argument for integrating feminist and social learning approaches when designing interventions in woman abuse. Pence and Shepard (1988) have offered a model of intervention based on a feminist analysis. And, as stated earlier, Carlson (1984) and Dutton (1985, 1988) have also previously applied an ecological framework to the same phenomenon. The integration of ecological, historical, feminist, and social learning approaches is evident throughout the literature on intervention with men who batter, yet few authors have explicitly made the connections we have here.

The overlaps between these approaches are clearly evident. For example, social learning theory and the ecological framework both view behavior as influenced by a unique set of events originating in a variety of systems. Feminist and social learning approaches both view violent behavior as functional and used by the man to gain concessions from his woman victim. Both approaches also view elimination of physically violent and psychologically abusive behavior as critical to any successful intervention. And, finally, changing the social structure that maintains violence against women is, or can be, a major focus of all three approaches. Throughout this book, we will make the advantages of combining these approaches explicit.

There are, of course, a variety of views concerning the development and maintenance of woman abuse. For example, some authors have proposed psychoanalytic approaches (McLeer, 1988) while others have argued for systemic models (Lane & Russell, 1989; Neidig & Friedman, 1984). We have selected approaches that, when combined, appear to offer the greatest explanatory power.

In the following chapters on assessment and intervention, we will apply this integrated approach. While we have introduced a range of technical terms in this chapter, we will only occasionally use them in later chapters to avoid becoming overburdened by jargon. The integrated framework is, however, present throughout the book. It is the foundation upon which both assessment and intervention rest. As such, we will examine working directly within a variety of microsystems consisting of individuals, families, and groups as well as discussing mesosystem and exosystem intervention through large-scale social systems.

3

Ecological Assessment of Men

The ecological assessment process includes not just a consideration of maltreating behavior and individual characteristics of the batterer but also an assessment of relevant factors in the social environment. In the assessment process, the data gathered inform decisions about the need for concurrent treatment and for individualization of the treatment program, among other needs. Practitioners must pay special attention to the danger of further violence. We highlight this aspect of assessment below.

Generally, the bulk of assessment takes place in initial intake sessions with individual violent men. Programs vary in the number of intake sessions, ranging from one to as many as four (Saunders & Hanusa, 1986). While initial intake sessions provide the opportunity for assessment, it is also during these sessions that some beginning efforts at intervention take place (e.g., contracting and safety planning, described in Chapter 4). Extensive crisis intervention may also occur in these initial sessions (Stordeur & Stille, 1989).

Assessment may begin with initial interviews but the need for assessment continues throughout the intervention process regardless of its form. Generally, men may become more forthcoming about their abusive behavior as they progress through the intervention process (Edleson & Brygger, 1986).

Ecological assessment also entails gathering information from other relevant data sources. One crucial source of information is the man's partner. Contacts with men's partners also start during assessment and extend throughout intervention. Partner contacts often modify initial impressions and data gathered directly from the man. Guidelines for involving men's partners in a safe manner are discussed later in this chapter. Data gathering will also extend to other systems the man is involved with, notably the criminal justice system and other helping professionals.

Assessment sessions with men use interview data as well as data from structured checklists like those listed later in this chapter. Generally, we gather interview and some checklist data during face-to-face interview sessions. Some paper-and-pencil measures may be filled out prior to or after face-to-face assessment sessions or in special times set aside for filling out the forms.

Assessment with men who batter must address a number of issues. When assessment is completed, the practitioner should have a good description of the abuse, clarifying issues like the frequency, severity, and chronicity of abuse. The information gathered in assessment yields not just an individual portrait of the client but a dynamic understanding of his relationship to the individuals and institutions in his social environment. The interrelationships and linkages between those in the man's environment, his mesosystem, must also be clarified. With this information, the ecological assessment can guide both the direct intervention with the man himself as well as identify the targets for intervention in the social environment. For example, contacts with a man's probation officer during assessment may reveal that the probation officer does not take the battering behavior very seriously. The practitioner thus becomes aware of the need to expend additional effort to make sure the man is properly monitored by the court system. Table 3.1 outlines the topics that are addressed in an ecological assessment.

Table 3.1   Outline of Assessment Topics

Nature of abuse:
  frequency
  chronicity
  severity
  types (e.g., physical, psychological, sexual)
  injury inflicted
  other targets of abuse (family members, outside the family)
  violence in the family of origin (observed, victim)
  type of denial
  agreement of corroborating sources
Individual characteristics:
  behavioral deficits
  depression
  hostility
  alcohol and drugs
  sex roles and attitudes
  psychopathology
  reading level
  intelligence
  language skills
Environmental factors:
  current living situation (e.g., separated, living together)
  social network (e.g., supportive of abusive behavior)
  external stressors
Likelihood of follow-through:
  level of remorse
  desire to reunite with partner
  involvement with criminal justice system
  effectiveness and saliency of external motivators
  match of program with client ability
  cultural sensitivity of program
Current risk of violence:
  increased frequency or severity of violence
  implicit or explicit threats
  client concern about ability to control himself
  use of alcohol or drugs
  availability of weapon
  history of weapon use
  past history of abuse
  level of denial
  violence normalized in employment setting
  pronounced psychological disturbance
  recent separation
  custody decisions

❑ Assessing Maltreatment

Intervention with men who batter primarily seeks to help men stop their abusive behavior. Accordingly, a major emphasis in assessment is an exploration of the ways in which a man has been abusive. Initial assessment sessions should provide the practitioner with sufficient information about the abusive behavior to make preliminary decisions regarding an individual's suitability for intervention and to develop a workable intervention plan. During initial assessment sessions, intervention begins as information about abusive and violent behavior is provided and men are confronted with their abusive behavior. For example, when men are asked to comprehensively describe their abuse behavior and its consequence, they may become more aware that they need to change their destructive behavior. The questions about abusive behavior asked in assessment begin to educate men about what types of behavior are of concern to the program. Often, men come in defining abuse as punching or beating up a woman. If the practitioner explicitly asks about a wide range of physically and psychologically abusive behaviors, the practitioner may increase the range of behaviors a man considers to be abusive.

Structured checklists may be useful for assessing the range and frequency of abusive behaviors. These checklists are generally integrated into the intake sessions themselves rather than being administered separately. This allows for a dynamic discussion of the maltreatment reported and allows the practitioner to probe for information that may be lacking from structured checklists. The most widely used measure is the Conflict Tactics Scale (Straus, 1979). The CTS lists a number of abusive behaviors and asks men to rate how often they occur. Most of the items of the CTS focus on physical abuse (e.g., grabbing, pushing, shoving, slapping, punching). Six items have been used to measure what Straus et al. (1989) label as verbal/symbolic aggression. These items include insulted or swore at him or her, sulked and/or refused to talk about it, stomped out of the house or yard, did or said something to spite him or her, threatened to hit him or her or throw something at him or her, threw or smashed or hit or kicked something. Variations of the CTS that expand the number of abusive behaviors monitored are in wide use. For example, one in use by the Domestic Abuse Project in Minneapolis adds a number of behaviors not included on the original CTS, including some psychological maltreatment items (threatened punishment other than physical such as withholding money) and some sexual abuse items (e.g., verbally pressured to have sex, physically forced sex) and additional physical abuse items (e.g., choked or strangled). When using these checklists interactively during the session, the practitioner can probe for contextual information about how and when the abusive behavior occurred and whether any injuries occurred as a result. This information is missed if the practitioner depends on checklists of abusive behavior alone.

Several checklists have been developed for more extensive assessment of psychological maltreatment. The Index of Spouse Abuse (Hudson & McIntosh, 1981) consists of 30 items that measure both physical and nonphysical abuse. Its usefulness for assessing men who batter is limited in that it is worded for use only by their partners. Male self-report cannot be measured by the ISA. The Psychological Maltreatment of Women Inventory (Tolman, 1988) is a 58-item scale that includes a broad sample of behaviors that do not appear on the CTS or ISA. The PMWI has parallel forms for men and women to fill out. Similar in format to the ISA, the PMWI asks clients to report on the relative frequency of each behavior that has occurred. Two factor-analytically derived subscales measure dominance-isolation and verbal-emotional abuse with satisfactory reliability. Preliminary validation work demonstrates that the number of acts endorsed, and summative scores of both the dominance-isolation and the verbal-emotional subscales, successfully discriminate battered from nonbattered women (Tolman, 1991).

> *Logs require men to monitor incidents in which they use coercive or abusive behavior.*

Other monitoring measures such as critical incident logs are often used on an ongoing basis in the assessment and treatment of abusive men. Critical incident logs have various names in the literature including "anger logs," "control logs," and "violence reports." While significant differences in treatment theory are reflected in the different names, logs usually require men to monitor incidents in which they use coercive or abusive behaviors. Such logs can be an important source of information about the use of physical and psychological maltreatment. Because men tend not to be forthcoming about their abusive behavior early, at intake, ongoing assessment using logs can be an important aspect of the intervention process.

Other qualitative approaches may also be helpful when gathering information about a man's abusive behavior. One strategy for getting a qualitative view of the nature of a man's abusive behavior is to ask him about the first, worst, and most recent examples of his abusive behavior. These are chosen because they may be most readily recalled, they may hold symbolic importance, and they may reveal themes and issues in the abuse. Often, the worst incident is one of the most recent as well and may be the reason that a man is seeking assistance at this time.

DENIAL

Men who batter characteristically attempt to deny or excuse their abusive behavior in a number of ways (Adams & McCormick, 1982). Men may minimize their abusive behavior or the effects of their behavior. "I only slapped her once (when he actually punched her repeatedly). "She only had a slight bruise" (when her jaw was broken). "I just lightly grabbed her wrist, but she bruises easily." Some men completely deny that they were in any way violent, claiming their partners are making it up or imagining the abuse. Some admit to their actions but rationalize the circumstances or meaning of their behavior. He may claim his actions were legitimate discipline of his wife or an attempt to calm her down. A man may blame his partner. "She goaded me into it." "She pushed my buttons, she knows exactly how to get me worked up." He may place the blame on external factors or circumstances, such as alcohol or drug use or job stress.

The strength of his denial may be an important factor in predicting his chances of success in the program. Generally, if a man completely denies any problems with abusive behavior, we will not accept him for intervention. Because intervention is geared toward helping work through his denial, however, we generally do not demand a high degree of personal responsibility for abuse during initial assessment sessions. These sessions do provide a forum, however, for beginning the process of confrontation that will help him become more accountable for his behavior.

The assessment should begin building a Workable relationship between practitioner and client.

While confrontation and its place in intervention are discussed more fully in Chapter 4, it is important to clarify some aspects of the role of the practitioner during assessment as well as the practitioner's relationship with the client. With the emphasis on determining the facts about a man's abusive behavior, and the expectation that the man is not likely to be forthcoming in his accounts of his behavior, it is easy to imagine that assessment sessions could take on the character of a hostile interrogation. The assessment process must not be one in which the practitioner badgers the man for details, accuses him of lying, and triumphantly produces third-party reports that show the man he has been trapped by the evidence. Rather, the assessment should begin building a workable relationship between practitioner and client. This relationship must balance support and confrontation. The practitioner must set limits without being punitive and empathize with the client without excusing his actions. The practitioner depends on supportive confrontation as the primary tool (EMERGE, 1981), in which empathy for the client can be balanced with nonpunitive confrontations that challenge him to view his behavior differently.

DATA FROM PARTNERS

Because men who batter tend to minimize, deny, and distort their own abusive behavior, other sources of data must also be used to achieve a full and accurate assessment. Other sources include the man's partner as well as police and court records. Data from women partners may be gathered in separate individual sessions or by telephone at the outset of treatment. Because of safety considerations, as well as the likelihood of data being distorted (see Chapter 5), partner reports should not be gathered in the presence of the batterer. Safety checks with female partners can be used on an ongoing basis throughout intervention to check on the reliability of men's reports of their abusive behavior as well as to reach out to women who may be in danger. Care must be taken at every step not to inadvertently place a woman at risk by revealing what she says about her partner's abusive behavior without her careful and informed consent. Sometimes even when a woman gives permission to confront her partner with a discrepancy between his reports of abuse and her own, program staff may decide that such a confrontation would be too risky. Hart (1988) argues that ensuring the safety of battered women whose partners are participating in a men's program requires close monitoring on a program level. That is, the battered women's advocates must work closely with those delivering men's programs to ensure that the philosophy, goals, and curricula clearly aim to end violence and guarantee victim safety, and methods for judging a batterer nonviolent must be clearly established. She also suggests that battered women's advocates be involved in sharing comprehensive information about the program and an individual batterer's progress with the woman partner. Such a collaboration between advocates, battered women, and program staff may offer new opportunities for feedback to the men's program and greatly enhance victim safety planning. Providing women victims with complete and ongoing information about their partners' program may also lessen any power a man might try to gain by withholding information or manipulating its meaning for use against his partner.

Stordeur and Stille (1989) discuss the need for caution in what is included in case records and assessments about the information partners provide, because at some point the man may have access to the reports and punish his partner for her disclosures. By having regular contacts with the women throughout, we minimize men's distortion of intervention (e.g., "avoiding" violence by leaving for 3 days) and enhance our ability to assist women when and if we invoke "duty to warn."

While the field has developed various measures of physical violence and psychological maltreatment, the impact of such behaviors has seldom been the focus of measurement instruments. Saunders (1992) points out the need for an injury scale that systematically documents the physical impact of violence.

VIOLENCE AGAINST OTHERS

A critical assessment area concerns violence or other abusive behavior directed at children. Assessment of child maltreatment can begin with an assessment of general parenting behaviors and a discussion of the client's relationship with his children.

Often, a discussion of disciplinary techniques reveals a pattern of abusive treatment. For example, one study found that many batterers may also be sexually abusing their children (Truesdell, McNeil, & Deschner, 1986). While men are not likely to reveal such abuse at an early stage in treatment, contacts with partners and children often lead to revelations about sexual abuse.

When child maltreatment is revealed, reports must be made to the proper child protection authority. This raises confidentiality concerns, which some programs have addressed by describing the limits of confidentiality prior to gathering intake information. Men may reveal abuse of the children by their partner during intake as well. Practitioners should be wary of such reports, which may be a manipulative attempt to punish his partner by taking the children away from her. As it generally is impossible to be sure this is the case during an intake session, a report will need to be filed regardless of one's suspicions that the report may later be dismissed. This makes availability of outreach and support for the partner critical, lest the man's involvement in a men's program creates additional opportunities for victimization of his partner.

A key personal chronosystem issue is the man's experience with violence in previous relationships and in his family of origin. His awareness that his current relationship is not the first in which he has been abusive may provide a key tool for confronting him about his responsibility for his violence.

At intake, men should also be asked about violence they have directed at others, including siblings, in-laws, other family members, friends, and coworkers as well as participation in any other violence (e.g., bar fights). Violence against others in addition to the man's current partner must be assessed for several reasons. First, others who may be in danger of the man's abuse should be identified, should the need to warn them become necessary. Ongoing safety checks with those people may be required. Research suggests that men who use violence both inside and outside the home use more severe violence (Fagan, Steward, & Hansen, 1983), exhibit greater drug and alcohol use, and have less stable relationships with lower commitment to them than do men violent toward their families alone (Shields, McCall, & Hanneke, 1988). Generally, violent men may pose the most difficult challenge for practitioners. And, generally, violent men with previous records of violent crime may be more likely to be involved in a criminal subculture that supports aggression and may find the threat of sanctions from the criminal justice system less credible (Fagan, 1989).

VIOLENCE IN THE FAMILY OF ORIGIN

The prevalence of experiencing violence in the family of origin among men who batter ranges from 24% (for nonalcoholic batterers; Hastings & Hamberger, 1988) to 81.1% (Roy, 1977). Observation of violence in the family of origin has more consistently predicted violence by men toward their partners than has abuse as a child (Hotaling & Sugarman, 1986).

The high prevalence of family of origin violence is consistent with a social learning analysis, which predicts that modeling of violence during childhood would increase the likelihood of the behavior later in life and supports a focus of intervention on alternative skills training. The high frequency of family of origin violence also suggests that intervention with men who batter should somehow address early victimization. Some men seem unaware of their victimization as children at assessment, but they may become more aware of their own victimization during the course of intervention for battering. This process may ultimately facilitate empathy for their victims, if men have the support to address their victimization issues without diminishing their responsibility for their own violent actions.

Screening assessments should explore the range of family of origin experiences. Violence between parents, other siblings, or other family members should be examined. Information about physical, psychological, and sexual maltreatment directed at the client should be sought. Sexual abuse as a child may be a risk factor for a man's sexual abuse of his children.

Studies of family of origin violence suggest some additional potential clinical applications. Family of origin violence discriminates woman batterers from men who are assaultive in general (Dutton, 1988; Shields et al., 1988), recidivate from nonrecidivate batterers (DeMaris & Jackson, 1987), alcoholic from nonalcoholic batterers (Hastings & Hamberger, 1988), and men who are severely violent from men who exhibited minor violence or were verbally aggressive with their partners (Hotaling & Sugarman, 1986). Therefore family of origin violence may be a factor in assessing for dangerousness and alcohol and drug abuse and in assessing the potential for treatment follow-through.

Some men who abuse their partners may also experience violence directed at them by their partners. Many others will describe a partner's use of force against him but distort the fact that her violence is self-defense or does not physically threaten him. Assessment of the abuse a man may have experienced from his partner is problematic because it may imply victim blaming or excusing his abuse. It is probably better for the practitioner to explicitly raise the issue of partner violence and draw the distinction between assessing this abuse and in any way excusing or justifying the man's behavior. For example, a practitioner might clarify the issue by telling a man that the program he will participate in expects that he will learn skills for dealing with the most volatile of issues and that he will learn ways to handle those situations nonviolently. Even if his partner threatens him physically, he can find ways to respond nonabusively himself.

❑ Individual Characteristics

While battering itself is the focus of intervention, many individual characteristics of men may affect the course of intervention. Identification of characteristics that discriminate batterers from nonbatterers may increase the accuracy of prediction of recidivism and improve understanding of the causes or maintaining factors of woman abuse. The ability to use characteristics to define differential treatment strategies is not yet well developed, but the following section attempts to link some commonly noted individual characteristics of men who batter with their implications for the intervention process. The search for characteristics that differentiate men who batter from other men may cloud important similarities or societal conditions that make battering commonplace and tolerated. The identification of individual characteristics can usefully inform practice only if it does not obscure these other relevant levels of the ecology.

BEHAVIORAL DEFICITS

Research on behavioral deficits supports the belief that batterers may have assertiveness deficits (Douglas, Alley, Daston, Svaldi-Farr, & Samson, 1984; Maiuro, Cahn, & Vitaliano, 1986; Rosenbaum & O'Leary, 1981b). A study by Maiuro et al. revealed a more specific deficit than previously noted in the literature. They found batterers could effectively defend their rights and territory but had difficulty expressing their desires in a socially appropriate manner. Men with such deficits may require additional clinical attention because they may feel a greater loss of personal control and more vulnerability to rejection when attempting to express their needs.

Dutton and Strachan (1987) found that batterers had greater need for power than men without relationship problems but were equal to maritally distressed men in power needs. Abusers, however, were less assertive with their spouses than either group. This suggests that men who batter may view intimate relationships with women not only as dangerous but as uncontrollable. This combination may produce extreme anxiety and anger for men with high power needs; but, while both abusive and maritally conflicted men have high power needs, abusers have low verbal assertion and therefore could not satisfy their power needs verbally. They may then resort to violence.

These assertion studies indicate that assertion training, particularly targeted on the appropriate expression of requests or needs in a noncoercive and nonabusive manner, is a relevant focus of intervention with men who batter. Paper-and-pencil measures of assertion such as the Spouse Specific Assertion Scale (O'Leary & Curley,

1986) may prove useful in identifying men with specific assertiveness deficits.

DEPRESSION

Ganley and Harris (1978) suggest that the risk of serious depression and suicide among men who batter is high. Rosenbaum and Bennett (1988) propose that depressive affect associated with a sense of personal injury, especially due to real or imagined infidelity of a partner, may erupt explosively in violent and homicidal behavior. Our clinical experience suggests that, as men's hopelessness and depression increase, particularly when threatened with or experiencing a physical separation from a partner, men accelerate their attempts to control their partners.

The empirical evidence to date does suggest that depression is a factor for men who batter (Hamberger & Hastings, 1986; Maiuro, Cahn, Vitaliano, Wagner, & Zegree, 1988; Saunders & Hanusa, 1986). Hamberger and Hastings (1988) found no significant differences between undetected batterers in the community and a nonviolent comparison group on a depression scale, but nonalcoholic and alcoholic batterers in the clinical sample were significantly more depressed. For some men, depression may be a situational response to separation or other negative consequences of battering, such as criminal justice system consequences. Others may have more longstanding affective disorders.

When a man comes to intervention experiencing dysphoria due to separation from his partner, a supportive intervention environment may offer him hope and support in managing the depressed affect. That support, however, must be facilitative in linking his depression to the consequences of his abusive behavior. Replacing his abusive behavior with constructive alternatives may then become a key in overcoming his dysphoria. The ability to provide support while holding men accountable for their abusive behavior may be one element treatment programs offer that intervention strategies such as arrest do not. It is counterproductive, however, to empathically support batterers for their depression if it deflects interventive focus away from their abusive behavior (Adams, 1988). On the other hand, programs must be prepared to provide proper service or referral to men whose depression interferes with intervention or to men who may be suicidal or homicidal.

In addition to a clinical interview, some programs make use of assessment tools like the Beck Depression Inventory (Beck, Ward, Mendelson, Mock, & Erbaugh, 1961) to determine whether a man is depressed. More detailed histories must be gathered to determine the type of depression a man is experiencing, for example, whether it is related to the consequences of his battering or whether it has other origins.

HOSTILITY

Research suggests that men who batter are more hostile and angrier than nonviolent controls (Barnett & Planeaux, 1989; Maiuro et al., 1986; Maiuro et al., 1988). They do not, however, seem to differ from generally violent men (Maiuro et al., 1988) or maritally discordant men (Barnett & Planeaux, 1989). On the other hand, preliminary research evidence indicates that men who are physically abusive are more likely to feel angry in conflict situations or relationship anxiety situations than men who choose not to act violently (Dutton & Browning, 1987; Margolin, John, & Gleberman, 1988). Men who batter may have difficulty identifying emotions other than anger and may overlabel any type of negative affectivity as anger (Dutton, 1988).

The evidence supports the use of anger management techniques in intervention that focus on recognizing arousal cues, developing greater awareness of feelings, and relabeling or reframing arousal states experienced as anger. A practitioner, however, must attempt to assess the degree to which a man may self-generate anger to serve as a rationalization for his coercive behavior. Whether such anger is used as a rationalization or serves as a setting event that increases the probability of aggression, the belief that abuse is acceptable if one is angered must be challenged at assessment as well as in intervention.

Practitioners assessing anger and hostility may make use of the Buss-Durkee Hostility Inventory (Buss & Durkee, 1957); the Brief Anger-Aggression Questionnaire, a brief screening tool derived from the Buss-Durkee measure (Maiuro, Cahn, & Vitaliano, 1986); or the Novaco Anger Scale (Novaco, 1975).

ALCOHOL AND DRUGS

A review of the literature on alcohol and violence suggests that chronic alcohol abuse by the male rather than acute intoxication is a better predictor of battering and that perhaps half of all batterers coming to intervention are going to have alcohol abuse problems (see Tolman & Bennett, 1990). Programs for batterers must be prepared to treat or refer chemical dependence problems. The treatment for alcohol or drug problems must occur prior to or concurrently with the intervention for battering. There is no evidence that alcohol treatment in itself will be effective in changing abusive behavior, but alcohol and drug problems no doubt interfere with the process of such change (Maiuro & Wood, 1988).

Some programs use screening instruments to augment clinical histories of drug and alcohol use. The Michigan Alcohol Screening Test (Pokorny, Miller, & Kaplan, 1972) is one widely used measure. If staff making the assessments are not properly trained, it may be helpful to refer the man for an independent alcohol and drug assessment.

SEX ROLES AND ATTITUDES

Research suggests that batterers view themselves as low in masculinity and low in positive traits stereotypically associated with either gender (LaViolette, Barnett, & Miller, 1984; Rosenbaum, 1986). Men who believe they do not live up to societal notions about their gender role behavior may compensate through aggressive behavior toward their partners to bolster their masculine self-images. Findings support a focus on sex role resocialization in groups for men who batter.

Our assumption is that negative attitudes toward women that are promoted culturally contribute to the prevalence of woman abuse. Therefore the degree to which a man holds such negative attitudes is relevant to assessment. We have found, however, that the use of traditional instruments to measure attitudes toward women are not useful in assessment. Some men are quite overt in their attitudes, and an assessment instrument is not necessary. Most men tend to give the "right" answers on paper-and-pencil measures of attitudes toward women. Usually, their hostility and negativity to women comes out as the group progresses, in subtle and at times not so subtle ways. How practitioners can be alert to hearing the sexist assumptions that men hold is discussed in the next chapter.

PSYCHOPATHOLOGY

Studies suggest (Caesar, 1985; Faulkner et al., 1988; Hamberger, Hastings, & Lohr, 1988) that woman abuse is not limited to men with personality problems or other identifiable psychological problems. Men with psychological disorders do, however, seem to constitute a large proportion of the identified treatment population, especially among those men who have alcohol or drug problems (Hamberger et al., 1988). The overrepresentation of psychopathology in clinical samples does not mean that pathology is a causal factor in abuse. There are many reasons why more pathological men would be the ones to volunteer for or be mandated to treatment in greater numbers than other batterers. Batterers with psychological disorders may have a greater likelihood of detection or arrest by outside sources. They may be more amenable to treatment because of previous treatment experiences for their other problems (e.g., alcohol treatment or psychiatric care) or may seek intervention for reasons other than the battering. Regardless of whether there is a causal link to battering, men involved in intervention for battering may exhibit psychological problems that affect intervention.

Assessment of psychopathology may have important implications for service delivery but the usefulness of that information depends on how clearly differential intervention plans can be drawn from the assessment data. One problem is that useful differential treatments for identifiable subgroups of batterers are just being developed. Because many community-based programs emphasize structured group programs, and may not have resources to provide a full range of psychotherapy or other psychological services, identification of psychopathology is most likely to be useful in guiding decisions about the need for additional treatment and medication or to establish whether a particular man is suitable for a specific treatment program.

Identifying common personality patterns and clusters of problems may at some point lead to service configurations. Hastings and Hamberger (1988), for example, developed an empirical typology based on personality test data. Three major subgroup profiles emerged. The first profile, associated with the borderline personality disorder, describes an individual who is asocial, withdrawn, moody, and hypersensitive to interpersonal slights. A man with this profile is viewed by others as volatile and overreactive. He may vacillate from calm one minute to extreme anger in the next. The men in this group exhibit high levels of anxiety, depression, and alcohol problems.

The second profile, a cluster associated with narcissistic and antisocial personality disorders, describes a self-centered person who uses others to meet his needs and only reciprocates when it meets his advantage. Men with this profile insist their perceptions, values, and rules be accepted by others. Hesitation by others to respond to the self-centered man's demands violates his sense of entitlement to be treated according to his standards, and he responds with threats and aggression.

The third profile describes a tense, rigid individual who behaves in a passive or ingratiating manner and is associated with a dependent/compulsive personality cluster. These men lack self-esteem and have a strong sense of need for one or a few significant others. Rebellious hostile feelings can result from failure to meet those needs. The men in this group exhibited low anger and moderate depression. An understanding of these patterns may help in, among other things, prediction of situations in which men may be more likely to use abusive behavior, in identifying core cognitive patterns that may support their abuse, and in assessing the need for concurrent treatment.

Hamberger and Hastings (1990) found that men with a narcissistic profile were more likely to repeat abuse following treatment than men without such a profile. Changing personality disorders is beyond the scope of short-term intervention for batterers. More research will be certainly be needed on whether men with specific personality profiles can use the type of treatment resources generally available to batterers. As Gondolf (1988) points out, referring men whose violence may be relatively intractable to counseling may increase the likelihood of their partners remaining with them, thus raising women's hopes with little real possibility of change occurring and with the strong possibility of endangering them.

In assessing for psychological problems, a variety of tools may be used. Practitioners can gather a history that includes details about previous psychological treatment, family history of pathology, and any current involvement in psychological services.

Some authors recommend routine psychological testing at intake. Stordeur and Stille (1989) use the Minnesota Multiphasic Personality Inventory (Hathaway & Meehl, 1951) to identify general and pathological personality traits, defense patterns, level of distress, depression and anger, general ego strength, and level of identification with male roles. Hamberger, Hastings, and Lohr (1988) recommend routine psychological testing of men who batter at intake and use of the Millon Clinical Multiaxial Inventory (1983) for screening for personality disorders and other psychological problems.

READING ABILITY, INTELLIGENCE, LANGUAGE SKILLS

Structured group programs for men who batter, as described in Chapter 4, tend to depend on reading handouts and on completing homework assignments, tasks that create difficulties for men with poor language or reading ability or with low intelligence. This may explain why some studies find that men with lower education are less likely to complete programs (Grusznski & Carrillo, 1988; Saunders & Parker, 1989). Many men with reading problems often are ashamed to admit it and may try to hide the problem from program staff. Their inability to successfully complete assignments may be misinterpreted as resistance.

Assessment at intake for intelligence and reading ability may circumvent later problems. Men who have such problems may need special support in the program. For example, experienced members may be recruited to help them with their homework, or audiotapes may help with reading materials. Practitioners might use the Shipley Institute of Living Scale (Shipley, 1940), which Stordeur and Stille (1989) have recommended for quick use in assessment of intellectual functioning and as a measure of how much stress may be interfering with clients' abilities to solve problems or process thoughts.

❏ Microsystem Assessment

MAN'S LIVING SITUATION

Assessment of a man's current living situation, one of his most important microsystems, is obviously important for intervention. If he is not living with his partner, this may affect his motivation for change, depending on whether or not he hopes to reunite with her. While separation may be preferable as it may decrease access to his partner, and provide some safety, separation by no means is a guarantee that he will not abuse his partner. Frequently, undesired separations are the most volatile circumstances for men and may increase the risk for lethality (see below). Some men find themselves without a stable living situation, as they may have been ordered out of their homes by an order for protection and may need some help in working out adequate living arrangements. While the focus of work needs to remain on his responsibility for abusive behavior, supportive involvement in resolving these types of crises can both enhance the working alliance between client and practitioner and reduce the risk of abuse in the situation because the man finds a nonabusive method for meeting his needs in the crisis.

SOCIAL NETWORKS

Examination of the batterer's social network is important when determining the availability of resources for supporting his nonviolence and identifying barriers to his ability to change. Two specific network issues impinge directly on efforts to change battering. One is a lack of social support. When men are isolated, they may be overdependent on their partners for meeting all their emotional needs. How the social network supports or discourages abusive behavior affects a man's ability to change. Eisikovits, Guttmann, Sela-Amit, and Edleson (1991) found that many batterers were not isolated and had many contacts who supported their abusive behavior.

Several measures that assess social support networks have been used in studies of woman abuse. The Domestic Abuse Project in Minneapolis has used an 18-item questionnaire that is adapted from one initially reported in a study by Mitchell and Hodson (1983). The measure is designed to monitor changes in client social isolation and the quality of social contacts. Men estimate the frequency of social contacts they have with and without their partner present, indicate the number of friends and relatives they can talk to about personal problems, and rate 15 social contact items on a 5-point scale from "never" to "always." The measure yields two frequencies of social contacts (with or without partner), the number of people with whom he feels he can share personal problems, and three types of social contacts: those that support abuse, those that do not support abuse, or those that actively intervene to stop it.

A more complete measure of social support is the Interview Schedule for Social Interaction (ISSI). Developed by Henderson and his colleagues in Australia (Duncan-Jones & Henderson, 1978; Henderson, Duncan-Jones, Byrne, & Scott, 1980; Henderson, Duncan-Jones, Byrne, Scott, & Adcock, 1979), the 40-item ISSI provides a quantitative description of interpersonal relationships based on six benefits or provisions offered by a social network: attachment, social integration, nurturing, reassurance, reliability, and assistance.

EXTERNAL STRESS

Stressors in men's microsystems have not been generally viewed as directly causal of battering, but it has been argued that, in combination with other variables, stress may increase the likelihood of violence (Straus, 1980). Studies do not make a strong case for the role of external stress in battering (Hotaling & Sugarman, 1986). Barling and Rosenbaum (1986), for example, found that abusive men did not differ from nonabusive men on most of the measures of work stress used in their study. MacEwen and Barling (1988) studied working couples and found that life stress was not predictive of abuse.

While stress may not be causally linked to battering, problems in various microsystems may present the need for crisis intervention at intake. For example, a man with a seriously ill patient may be helped to arrange medical care and support services if needed.

❏ Likelihood of Follow-Through

An important decision facing practitioners is whether a man is a good risk for community-based service. One factor in making a decision about a man's suitability for such treatment is the likelihood of his following through with treatment. All of the external, internal, program, and other factors may influence his follow-through.

Practitioners generally view nonvoluntary clients as resistant to intervention (Rooney, 1988). Research assessing differences in characteristics of men court mandated and non-court mandated to treatment indicates that this distinction is not particularly relevant at assessment. To date, no evidence exists to support various types of court orders as having more impact on follow-through than others. Issues of assessing the effectiveness of the criminal justice system in getting men to follow through with treatment, and the factors involved in that effectiveness, will be discussed in Chapters 4 and 6.

Whether a man comes to intervention without court intervention may not actually be a good measure of "volunteerism." Some type of pressure has usually been placed on him to attend. A man's partner may threaten to leave if he does not seek help. She may already have left, and he is seeking help only to save the relationship (Bowker, 1982; Fagan, 1989). We do not refer to non-court-mandated men as voluntary but as "partner" or "socially" mandated to intervention. Rooney (1988) uses the term "mandated" for those clients whom the court sends and "nonvoluntary" for others who come through the influence of others.

Because the presence of court sanctions alone does not predict motivation, an assessment of the individual motivation of each client, and the role various consequences like court involvement might play on his continuing in a program, provide better guidance for intervention decisions. Among the factors that may predict a man's follow-through are his investment in maintaining a relationship with his partner and the degree of remorse he shows about his abusive behavior. Men who have initiated termination of the relationship with the battered woman may be less motivated to continue in the program. Often, men have begun relationships with new partners, and the initial romance of a new relationship may contribute to his shifting the responsibility for his abusive behavior to his former partner. For example, a man in one of our groups said he would not hit his new partner because she was understanding and did not communicate poorly like his former partner.

Men who show remorse for their behavior seemingly have more internal motivation for change. In one sense, remorse indicates that their capacity for self-punishment and self-regulation of their abusive behavior has not been completely neutralized (Bandura, 1973). One must be aware, however, that a man's expression of remorse may be primarily rhetorical, that is, meant to win back his partner, rather than truly experienced internally.

Research suggests that treatment may be less likely to effectively reach younger, less educated, lower income, and minority men (Saunders & Parker, 1989). The evidence that these men might not follow through suggests that programs need to make special efforts to reach them. As Saunders (1992) points out, we may mislabel clients as resistant when program factors have created the problem in motivation.

Maintaining some men's attendance requires special intervention. Some efforts to reduce attrition focus on pregroup preparation or orientation. Deschner and McNeil (1984) and Tolman and Bhosley (1991) each discovered that an intensive one-day workshop reduced the dropout rate in intervention groups for batterers. While these studies suggest that dropouts can be reduced by altering program structures, the studies were not particularly aimed at younger, less educated, or minority men in particular. Future exploration of treatment structure by client characteristic interactions are necessary to explore what intervention structures can reduce attrition for clients with special needs and issues.

☐ Assessing Dangerousness

Research indicates that the best predictor of future behavior is past behavior (Monahan, 1981). Men who batter have demonstrated that they present a risk of harm to their partners. This means programs must be structured in such a way as to provide as much safety as possible for partners and other potential victims, because any man is potentially dangerous. Nevertheless, we cannot ignore characteristics or circumstances that may lead us to warn potential victims or to take special precautions. Assessment of dangerousness is also necessary for those making decisions about whether men are appropriate for community-based treatment or whether jail or other sanctions are more appropriate. Unfortunately, research indicates that clinical models for predicting dangerousness have proven to be inaccurate. Statistical models have performed somewhat better but by no means can be characterized as satisfactory in predicting future violence (Gottfredson & Gottfredson, 1988; Quinsey & Maguire, 1986).

Despite these problems, practitioners must still attempt to make an assessment of clients' dangerousness. Sonkin (1988) identifies the following situations as cause to consider warning a potential victim of danger: when the frequency or severity of violence is increasing during treatment; when implicit or explicit threats are made; when the client is in crisis and cannot assure the practitioner that he is in control of himself; when the victim expresses a concern for her own safety or that of others; when the client's use of alcohol or drugs increases; when the client refuses to follow through with the intervention plan or aspects of it; when the client has not been open about acts of violence committed during intervention; or when it is discovered the client committed life-threatening violence or had made specific threats to kill prior to treatment. The practitioner should also consider the client's perception of the seriousness of the threat, his access to the victim, and the potential victim's view of the seriousness of the situation.

In addition to those listed above, Stordeur and Stille (1989) discuss other factors that may indicate an increased risk of lethality. One set of factors surrounds the man's past use of violence and his current plans. If a man has a specific plan to harm someone, risk is clearly present. The potential lethality of such a plan increases if it includes use of a weapon, especially one with a high potential for lethality (such as a gun) and if the weapon is readily available (e.g., he carries it around with him). A history of life-threatening violence, including use of lethal weapons, indicates greater dangerousness. The potential lethality of the current situation may be greater if it is similar to past situations where severe abuse has occurred or if the man has ever killed before. Dangerousness may be greater if a man has a history of employment or participation in settings where use of violence has been normalized (e.g., combat experience).

Stordeur and Stille also discuss several psychological factors that may be an indication of greater risk. Practitioners should be concerned about the potential for lethality, either homicide or suicide, if a man expresses hopelessness about the future and is unable to see any alternatives to the use of violence. Psychiatric disturbance, including pronounced disorders such as delusions, may be a risk factor. Extreme isolation and lack of support systems or supportive others may increase risk because men may lack the social resources who could be valuable in exploring alternatives to the use of violence (Stordeur & Stille, 1989).

Finally, several additional factors may be related to dangerousness. Our experience suggests that a recent undesired separation, finalization of a divorce, a change in custody arrangements limiting his access to his children and partner, or his ex-partner entering a new relationship may all be particularly volatile times.

The assessment of dangerousness must be ongoing throughout intervention. When a decision is made that a man is currently a threat to his partner, she must be warned (Sonkin, 1988). The *Tarasoff* decision and subsequent court cases have made it clear that it is the legal duty of the practitioner to exercise reasonable care to protect foreseeable victims from a danger of violence. To fulfill this duty, practitioners may need to warn the foreseeable victims, call police, hospitalize the client, or take other appropriate steps (Sonkin, 1988).

Safety of potential victims is enhanced if programs for men maintain regular contact with women victims. When ongoing contact has been established, notification of risk can be carried out in a safer manner, with discussion of resources and plans of action taking place with someone who has a trusting relationship established. Because a battered woman herself may minimize or deny the potential extent of the violence or risk to her, an ongoing relationship with staff of the program treating her partner may enhance her ability to hear the message of danger and encourage her to protect herself. Ideally, she has access to a program that coordinates closely with staff from the program giving service to her partner. Joint involvement with that staff may be helpful in communication of risk to her. Ongoing safety checks with the women throughout her partner's participation in the program allow for data gathering that may enhance assessments of dangerousness as well as building a relationship with her.

The issue of dangerousness clearly shows the need for an ecological perspective. Predicting a man's dangerousness is useless if the environment cannot be altered to better protect a potential victim. For a woman's safety to be enhanced, she must have resources to protect herself, including shelter and other supportive programs. The police and court system must be willing to follow through on protective actions, including arrest, issuing and enforcing orders for protection, and proper sentencing. The better the linkages between the various actors, the more effectively her safety can be protected. Issues of coordination of the various systems involved in enhancing women's safety will be discussed further in Chapter 6.

❏ Cultural Influences

We have found it important to be aware of cultural and class differences during both the assessment and the intervention phases. In assessment, it is important to be careful about possible misinterpretation of certain behaviors. For example, in many Native American cultures, it may be disrespectful to have direct eye contact with someone in a position of authority. It may also be the case that a Native American man will be less talkative than men of other cultures. While this is often culturally appropriate behavior in Native American societies, it could be misconstrued by a counselor from a different culture as withdrawn or even depressive behavior.

While cultural differences may play a role in enhancing intervention, it is important not to overemphasize them in terms of responsibility for abusive behavior. Rather than being reduced to a cultural relativism, an ecological view encourages a critical view of macrosystem issues. Therefore one would not accept battering, or factors supportive of it, just because it is culturally sanctioned. Rather, one would work to maximize the opportunities for men and women to develop more optimally in violence-free environments.

❏ Summary

This chapter has focused on a variety of assessment factors. Understanding these individual and ecological factors that may enhance and reduce the likelihood of successful intervention is critical to the success of any efforts with men who batter. Careful assessment leads to a determination of what intervention or combination of interventions are most appropriate in a given case or community. Identification of likely points of intervention leads to a variety of specific efforts that are the foci of the following chapters.

4

Group Intervention for Men Who Batter

This chapter presents an overview of small group intervention with men who batter. Although intervention with men takes place in a variety of ways, the field has adopted small group treatment as a primary modality. The reasons for this will be discussed below. First, we present an overview of the current approaches used with men who batter, with an emphasis on where group interventions fit in the range of interventions available. Next, we offer our rationale for working with men in groups. We then discuss a number of issues regarding key dimensions of the structure and format of those groups and then describe the types of intervention techniques commonly used in groups for men who batter. Throughout the descriptions, the ecological context of intervention will be considered. Finally, we review research that evaluates the effectiveness of group programs for men who batter.

❏ The Current Network of
Interventions with Men Who Batter

Before moving on to discuss group intervention, it is important to step back and assess the current type of interventions used with men who batter. Battered women became a focal point of the women's rights movement in the early 1970s. Society's inaction in response to a woman beaten or raped in her home was seen as a primary example of how women's rights were being violated. Using a model first developed in Britain, groups of women's activists formed collectives that provided safe home networks or shelters for battered women (see Schechter, 1982). Services for battered women have since expanded to include legal advocacy, job training, and second-stage housing among others.

In 1977, eight men who were friends of women's activists in the Boston area came together to form a men's collective called EMERGE (see Adams & McCormick, 1982). The friends of these men were frustrated that so many women with whom they were working in shelters were being abused when they returned home. In other cases, a violent man in the community was known to be moving from one relationship to another and abusing each new woman partner. EMERGE thus became one of the first organizations in the world to offer group treatment to men who batter.

The five years following the founding of EMERGE witnessed the establishment of several hundred group treatment programs for men who batter in North America (see surveys by Feazell, Mayers, & Deschner, 1984; Pirog-Good & Stets-Kealey, 1985). The sponsors of group treatment programs have varied a great deal. Some of the earliest programs were the sole offering of small collectives of men, such as EMERGE in Boston (Adams & McCormick, 1982) and MCAB in Albany, New York (Edleson, Miller, Stone, & Chapman, 1985). The earliest court-linked program was developed by Ganley (1981, 1987) in Washington State and her model was widely disseminated in the 1980s. Programs such as AMEND in Denver developed a coordinated network of trained and supervised independent counselors (Ewing, 1987; Ewing, Lindsey, & Pomerantz, 1984). Other men's group treatment programs were established as part of a larger family service agency or a mental health center (Saunders, 1982), were offered by battered women's shelters (Tolman, Beeman, & Mendoza, 1987), or became a major component of multiservice programs dealing exclusively with woman abuse (Brygger & Edleson, 1987).

Most current group treatment programs are psychoeducational with many having an underlying profeminist orientation to the problem. The programs vary in length but most are short term, ranging from 6 to 32 weeks in length (see Edleson & Syers, 1990; Eisikovits & Edleson, 1989). These programs often offer individual counseling to men as a supplement to group processes. It is surprising how few authors have reported interventions that focus solely on work with individual men who batter.

During the same period that men's group treatment programs were being established, the dramatic proliferation of family treatment models resulted in a few attempts at counseling couples and families in which men were abusing their partners (Coleman, 1980; Cook & Frantz-Cook, 1984; Geller, 1982; Geller & Walsh, 1977-1978; Margolin, 1979). Such interventions are clearly a small minority of those discussed in the published literature. Most current couple and family counseling programs are based on a family systems view but draw strongly on cognitive-behavioral intervention methods (see Eisikovits & Edleson, 1989).

The battered women's movement has long been focused on the sociocultural dimensions of violence against women. Shelters are most often viewed as social change organizations that not only provide individual women with protection but also work to change larger systems. The mere existence of a shelter could be said to offer a new option even to those women who do not use it and also to alert violent men that there are people in their community who see their behavior as illegal and are working to hold them accountable for it.

The feminist framework of the women's movement logically led to an examination of larger systems and, in the early 1980s, to an innovation commonly called "community intervention projects" (Pence, 1983, 1989; Soler, 1987). As a result of landmark lawsuits against police, pressure from women's and victims' rights advocates, and growing research evidence, many criminal justice systems began to change their responses to battered women. Current community intervention projects aim to coordinate the response of the numerous subsystems within the larger criminal justice system. Like all other types of intervention in woman abuse, such projects differ in terms of their sponsorship, how they intervene, and what they judge to be evidence of programmatic success (see Edleson, 1991b).

These three types of intervention with men who batter—men's groups, couple counseling, and community intervention projects— dominate the North American scene and are the focus in this book. They do not, however, exist in a vacuum. Each type of intervention discussed here is only one part of a larger network, the success of which depends on the availability of an even larger set of services for battered women and their children.

❑ **Rationale for Group Intervention**

The group addresses the ecology of battering in a more direct way than may individual treatment. Although many men who batter express regret about their behavior, they are given mixed messages by those around them or even messages of direct support for their abuse of women. Through the group, the man's social networks expand to include others who

> *The group addresses the ecology of battering more directly than individual treatment.*

may be supportive of him becoming nonabusive. When other men in the same situation say, "I don't like what I am doing and I want to stop," a man struggling to be nonabusive will feel support rather than derision for his choice. Men may feel more confident in challenging others in their environment who promote abuse directly or indirectly (e.g., by putting down women) when they have the support of other men in the group. The group format is also beneficial in that it offers a variety of models and sources of feedback for men learning to self-observe, change cognitions, and interact differently (Rose, 1989). The group format also addresses the shame men feel about their behavior. When men self-disclose about their abuse in front of other men, and in an environment that supports their honest appraisal of their actions, their shame is reduced. By reducing this shame, men become more willing to own up to their behavior and to have the courage to change it.

At its best, a group offers men a set of relationships that reduces their dependence upon their partners for meeting all their emotional needs. The small group also provides men an opportunity to be helpful and supportive of others. When they become teachers, they not only are helping others but also are likely to reinforce their own learning.

In a follow-up study of a program for men who batter, Gondolf (1985) found that men ranked the group support as the most important element in helping them to stop their violence. Similarly, Tolman (1990) found that men reported the group itself as an important ingredient in bringing about change. Men talked about the group helping them feel less alone and about how hearing other men's stories and situations helped them to learn to cope more effectively, which supported their changing behavior.

Although men report positive views of being in groups, potential negative group effects exist. Men may find themselves angered by material discussed in the group. Sometimes group members support each other's negative attitudes about women or implicitly or explicitly support a man's use of abusive behavior. In the Tolman study, some women partners reported negative group effects. One woman said her husband came home and told her she should stop complaining because other men beat their wives much worse than he did. Another said her husband was angered by the complaints other men made about their partners and came home and harassed her. The potential for such negative male bonding in abuser groups calls for careful monitoring by group leaders and a willingness to confront these processes when they arise (Hart, 1988).

❑ Key Dimensions of Group Intervention

Groups for men who batter vary on several key dimensions. These include whether intervention is framed as education or therapy, the structure of the group, whether membership is open ended or closed ended, the length of the group, and what type of agency sponsors the group.

THERAPY OR EDUCATION

Groups for men who batter vary in the degree to which they are characterized either as therapy or as education. Several important implications arise from the manner in which intervention is framed. Therapy implies that the men have psychological problems that must be alleviated through treatment. As discussed in the assessment section, some men who batter do seem to suffer from a variety of diagnosable psychological problems. An ecological approach, however, with its attention to social as well as psychological causes of battering, must be attentive to the possible effects of labeling and the false emphasis labels may give to the causal contributions of intrapersonal factors while ignoring other social factors.

Framing intervention as education promotes the idea that men can learn to change, that they are not faulty individuals but men who have learned destructive messages about how to treat their intimate partners. This need not imply that therapy does not play a role in change for some men or even that many of the activities that take place in groups are not also "therapy." Framing intervention as education also seems to have the added benefit of reducing men's resistance to participation in the groups (Edleson & Syers, 1990).

STRUCTURE OF GROUPS

Structure refers to the degree that group activities are "programmed" in advance rather than emerging from the unique interests and dynamics of the group itself. Structuring groups for men who batter often means that agendas for each session are devised in advance and that the manner in which the session is conducted is predetermined. For example, a period of checking in about one's week is followed by a leader's presentation of material, group roleplays, and then time for group sharing.

Group structure may vary as a function of group development. For example, Stordeur and Stille (1989) describe a group that is highly structured at the outset of intervention but that moves to relatively less structured sessions in the final phases of the group. Advantages of structure include keeping a focus on abuse as the primary issue to be discussed, teaching important safety skills in an organized, clear fashion, ensuring coverage of important material, and limiting a propensity for negative male bonding.

Jennings (1987) has, on the other hand, argued that structure might actually interfere with effective intervention. He believes that the key issues covered in a structured group will emerge naturally from a group and that these self-generated group processes will increase men's motivation to change and provide greater opportunities for problem solving, development of peer support, and constructive confrontation. Rigidly overstructuring groups may interfere with these processes. Too much dependence on the leaders for structure can limit empowerment of the group members. Rigid methods, especially those applied in a harsh or punitive manner, may be perceived as authoritarian and increase men's unwillingness to participate. Too great a focus on structure may also limit discussion that might otherwise uncover other issues related to abuse. On the other hand, a structure that is too loose may pose a greater danger for a deviant group culture to form. If antisocial group norms develop, then the group may increase the chances for negative effects.

The relevant question probably is not structure or lack of it but whether a particular group helps men become accountable for their abuse and helps them learn ways to become nonabusive. We favor the structured approach because in our view it is more readily taught to others, lends itself more readily to outside scrutiny, and can be effectively administered by leaders who may not have the degree of group skill necessary to safely and effectively promote these goals in a unstructured environment. Even with that preference, however, most structured groups have unstructured components in each session (e.g., time for personal sharing), and the degree of structure tends to lessen as men move through the stages of group programs. Ultimately, men may move into relatively unstructured "after-care" self-help groups that capitalize on the positive processes that Jennings (1987) describes.

CLOSED VERSUS OPEN MEMBERSHIP

Some programs exclusively use a closed membership structure in which members begin and end their group experience together in a specified number of sessions. Open-ended groups incorporate new members into existing groups as other members leave.

Stordeur and Stille (1989) describe a closed-ended membership approach. Some programs have a two-step program in which men participate in an intensive closed and structured group and then "graduate" to an open, less structured group.

The open group structure has the advantage of using the growing expertise and comfort of existing members to challenge and support new members entering the group. In an open group, existing members often take more responsibility for orienting new members, taking over teaching tasks informally, and confronting the initial denial and minimization of new members. On the negative side, adding members to a group can be disruptive to group process by reducing the trust level. Energy must be taken from existing members and put into orienting the new members. Knowledge in the group is not at an equal level and so psychoeducational content must be repeated for the new members to learn the needed information.

Despite the disadvantages, many programs do not have the staff or enrollment to justify numerous closed membership groups. With limited staff, closed-ended groups can mean long waiting periods as new clients wait for existing groups to finish. Fortunately, there are methods for overcoming the difficulties of open membership groups.

One technique is the orientation group or orientation workshop. Prior to entering an open group, men participate in an orientation where they receive information regarding group rules, discuss how to be an effective group member, and are instructed in key content areas that allow them to more immediately function in the group. Initial reluctance may be addressed in orientation sessions, resulting in fewer disruptions when new members enter an open group. The research to date supports the use of such preparation in reducing attrition from groups (Deschner & McNeil, 1986; Tolman & Bhosley, 1991).

It is also possible to reframe some of the disadvantages of open groups in a positive way. For example, repetition of psychoeducational material may enhance learning and mastery of concepts. Our experience with groups is that, even though material may have been repeated, the men do not respond as if they have heard it all before.

Fresh examples and insights frequently arise from the men who had heard the material before. They are often more receptive to techniques the second time through and may be able to discuss problems or successes in implementation that also help other group members. Experienced members may also take more responsibility for teaching, in that they have been exposed to the material before. As a result, leadership of the group may become more shared and the development of protherapeutic norms enhanced.

TIME-LIMITED VERSUS OPEN-ENDED GROUPS

Programs vary widely in the sessions required of participants. Generally, batterers' groups meet once or twice a week for approximately 2 hours. Most group programs generally range from 10 to 30 sessions in length with some even shorter and others much longer (Eddy & Myers, 1984).

To date, there is no evidence to support long-term treatment over short-term treatment. In fact, our data (Edleson & Syers, 1990, 1991) suggest that they may be equal in efficacy. Brief, time-limited treatment has also been found to be as effective as longer treatment in a variety of other types of intervention (see Butcher & Koss, 1978; Videka-Sherman, 1988). It is a common experience for an individual to apply greater effort as a deadline approaches. It is also more likely that men will complete a shorter group program, thereby gaining reinforcement for having "graduated." Short-term treatment also has the obvious benefit of being more cost-effective and allowing limited resources to support intervention with larger numbers of men.

In spite of these advantages, several key arguments can be made in favor of longer group participation. It can extend treatment through important phases in the violence cycle whereas shorter groups may only be long enough for a man to make an initial attempt to stop his abuse and convince his partner to return. A longer group creates a different type of laboratory for change; it is harder for men to hide behind "nice guy" images; substance abuse issues may emerge and be confronted; and more intensive relationships may be formed. If a man remains in group through a longer period, he may receive support in maintaining his nonviolence during critical tests of his new skills. The increased time in a long-term group may provide an opportunity for repeated application of skills and repeated confrontation of sexist attitudes or lack of responsibility for violence. Finally, longer participation allows for the introduction of more material and coverage of relevant topics, such as focus on family of origin issues and nonabusive parenting that may not fit into the structure of a shorter-term group. If too much information is introduced in a group, however, the major points may be lost in an overabundance of material. While these advantages may exist, current data do not support the advantage of one length over another.

AGENCY AUSPICES

The context in which groups are offered may have important implications for service delivery. Groups may take place in programs exclusively for men who batter, such as EMERGE in Boston (Adams & McCormick, 1982). Shelters and other programs for battered women include men's groups as part of their comprehensive interventions (Brygger & Edleson, 1987). Men's groups also occur directly through the court system in many areas. In Illinois, the Cook County Court, through its social service department, works with several hundred men a year who have a court mandate to participate. Community mental health agencies and family service agencies, among others, now include men's groups in their available services. Private practitioners also now offer groups as do some self-help groups led by former batterers.

Programs located in very different settings often use similar intervention approaches (Eddy & Myers, 1984). However similar the content and structure of different groups may be, the interface between the program and those serving battered women in other key institutions such as the criminal justice system constitutes a key variable. In ecological terms, these linkages concern the mesosystem and, while such coordination requires time and effort, we see it as critical to the success of the program. The further a program is organizationally situated from key systems, the more crucial it is to develop ongoing linkages that improve that coordination. Chapter 6 discusses models of community linkages more extensively, as does Hart (1988).

❏ Group Intervention

The ecological perspective implies that intervention through men's groups will be aimed at multiple systems. There are three broad categories of procedures that are often used in groups: (a) altering attitudes toward violence and personal responsibility, (b) planning for safety, and (c) learning alternative skills for nonviolence. These procedures draw on a variety of group treatment models, often achieve multiple purposes, and are used in a variety of sequences.

ALTERING ATTITUDES

A variety of new skills are offered in men's groups but, in order for these techniques to be applied, group members must make the choice to use them. Men often begin a group in a state of denial. They see their partner, the police, or others as the source of their problem. Seldom do they attribute their current difficulties to their own violent or abusive behavior. To change their behavior, men must recognize and acknowledge their abusive behavior and have a full understanding of the effect it has on their partners, their relationships, and themselves.

Men must take responsibility not only for their overt physical violence, but for all their abusive behavior.

Expanding definitions. Men must take responsibility not only for their overt physical violence but for all their abusive behavior. It is important to expand their definitions of abuse to include a wide variety of physical violence and psychological maltreatment. This focus begins early, in intake when assessment focuses men on these behaviors. In the group, this focus is reinforced when the goals and purposes of the group are discussed. We have used an inductive exercise where men name behaviors they consider abusive and continue brainstorming until it includes a more broad-based definition of abuse. Critical incident logs are used to record the events surrounding violent incidents, and men are asked to complete a form each week describing their use of any controlling behaviors.

Pence (1989) describes a group curriculum in which various forms of abuse (physical abuse, nonphysical threats, economic abuse, use of male privilege, sexual abuse, isolation, and using children) are illustrated in the group via the use of a training video and the *Power and Control Wheel*. Men are then asked to identify their own use of those abusive behaviors. Subsequent sessions focused on each form of maltreatment and the development of alternative skills. The idea inherent in this discussion of expanding notions of abuse is that men must also expand their notions of responsible behavior.

Empathy. Groups aim, in part, to help men to move from denial to full empathy for their partners. Through structured exercises, and ongoing confrontation and support from leaders and members, this critical process moves forward.

An exercise that can help increase empathy is one that focuses on the costs and benefits of the man's behavior. In this exercise, men are asked to list the positive and negative effects of their behavior. A handout is provided listing additional possible effects. We have found that this exercise can be enhanced by showing a film that depicts the negative consequences prior to the exercise, such as *Up the Creek* (O.D.N. Productions, 1981). Men will often easily identify the obvious negative consequences, such as court involvement and separation, but find it more difficult to discuss the benefits of their behavior. Adams (1989) points out that men's professed ignorance about the effects of their abusive behavior allows them to focus on their good intentions in a situation. For example, a man may claim his abusive behavior was appropriate discipline for his wife or that he was only forcefully trying to get his point across to a partner who would not listen.

Addressing the consequences of abuse makes it clear that a man is responsible for those consequences despite his intentions. Adams (1989) also points out that exposing the hidden benefits of his abusive behavior makes it more difficult to maintain destructive behaviors once they are seen as calculated.

The goal of such empathy exercises is that men will come to see the hidden trap of their behavior, that negative consequences are more remote in time, and that the benefits accrue more immediately. In our experience, the most poignant moments early in group sessions are often those in which men realize, and express their dismay at, the paradox of their behavior. Their abusive and controlling behavior erodes the caring and closeness of their partners that they are so often desperately seeking to maintain through violence. Listing the benefits of abuse can help a man to identify what he really wants in a situation and to better identify and adopt strategies to meet those needs without violating the rights of his partner.

Another powerful exercise that helps men take responsibility is the report of each man's most violent incident. In this exercise, men identify their most abusive incident, describe it in detail to the group, and identify the points at which they chose to use physical and psychological abuse. They review the costs and benefits of that incident and discuss alternative behaviors they might have used rather than the abuse. This also serves as an opportunity to review safety planning techniques. The exercise asks them to identify what they really wanted during the incident. This is particularly helpful in identifying their expectations of their partners and the entitlements they feel in the relationship. When disclosed in the group, dysfunctional and sexist expectations can be confronted by leaders and members.

Confrontation. Confrontation by group members and leaders constitutes an important tool for promoting personal responsibility. Confrontation may be very direct or subtle, and it occurs at vir- tually all stages of men's involvement in groups. Confrontations may be directed at negative or sexist attitudes, support for abusive behaviors, and denial of abuse.

Sexist attitudes may be expressed in statements or behavior that reflect beliefs that women are not equal to men, that women have inherently negative qualities, or of "sexist" entitlements, that is, that women have obligations to men by virtue of their gender rather than equality within a relationship. For example, in a recent session, one man commented that his wife was "cheap" and that he was hiding resources from her so that he could spend them on himself. Another man followed with: "Yeah, they are all after your money." The second man was confronted for making a sexist generalization about women and about how this kind of comment was harmful to the man who was trying to examine his own actions with his wife. It diverted his and the group's attention away from the man's behavior and implied that the real problem rested in "women's nature." The group was then refocused on examination and confrontation of the first man's manipulation of financial resources. The need to discuss openly and negotiate resources in the relationship was noted.

Male socialization. Edleson et al. (1985) suggest a multistage exercise focused on enhancing men's awareness of their own socialization and how it affects their notion of success in relationships. In one session, the group leaders facilitate a group discussion of alternatives to violence and psychological maltreatment. The members are asked to generate as many nonviolent ways to communicate their feelings and to resolve conflicts with their female partners. In this and subsequent brainstorming, two rules are followed: (a) the more ideas the better, and (b) ideas are not discussed or evaluated until after the brainstorming time is over.

In the next session, the group leaders facilitate another group brainstorm on those men in the group members' lives who have acted as the role models on which they have styled their own lives. These are often celebrities, sports stars, and people closer to their personal lives. The names of role models are listed on newsprint taped to the wall. Once the role models have been listed, leaders ask group members to examine each role model and to identify the qualities of each person on the list that make him a role model. This process is often very revealing as the qualities usually include "strong," "successful," "woman's man," "macho," and the like.

Finally, after qualities have been attached to all the role models, both lists are compared with the prior week's list of nonviolent alternatives for communicating and resolving conflict. It is often the stark contrast between these nonviolent alternatives and the qualities of the men's role models that raises group members' awareness about their socialization and how it has artificially constrained their choices in relationships. The discussions that follow and the heightened awareness of how they have been trained to think about women and their relationships with them can be a very important moment for many group members.

Several variations on this exercise have also been successfully used in groups. One is to list all the words used to describe teenage boys or men who are sexually active and then to put up a second sheet of newsprint and to ask the men to list all the words used to describe teenage girls or women who are sexually active. This exercise clarifies the pervasive sexism in U.S. culture.

INCREASING AWARENESS

Frequently, men report that they suddenly find themselves in a rage. They report violence occurring almost spontaneously, without warning. Experience suggests that, when men begin to explore the chain of events leading to a violent incident, they begin to acknowledge that many physiological, cognitive, and situational cues were available to warn of a potential for violence. In addition, they come to realize that there were many points in that chain at which they could have acted in a way that might have prevented their violent behavior.

A set of interlocking procedures help men learn to control acute arousal that may precede abusive incidents. Planning for safety requires that men learn to self-monitor cues for arousal, interrupt the pattern of escalation, and somehow decrease that arousal to reduce the risk of violent behavior.

Self-monitoring. An early step in learning to monitor oneself is to understand the progression of violence. Many programs use Walker's (1979) "cycle of violence" framework to explain how situations escalate to violence and what occurs after the violent event. Walker states: "The battering cycle appears to have three distinct phases, which vary in both time and intensity for the same couple and between different couples. These are: the tension-building phase; the explosion or acute battering incident; and the calm, loving respite" (p. 55).

Our experience leads us to believe that, over time, the calm, loving respite phase of Walker's model will often disappear leaving women and child victims to experience only the tension-building and acute phases. For this reason, programs like the Domestic Abuse Project have relabeled Walker's model the "progression" of violence and view this progression as an ever rising level of tension with fewer and smaller dips or respites over time.

Following a didactic presentation of the progression of violence, group members are taught to identify the emotional, cognitive, and situational cues that portend their use of violence. Each man is first asked to identify and list his own cues during the tension-building phase. To increase each man's understanding of his partners' experience, he is also asked to identify what his partner might be doing, thinking, and feeling and how she might be trying to cope during the tension building. Men are also encouraged to look beyond individual acts of violence to the terror-filled environment they may have created. By doing so, they are encouraged to reexamine how threats and other forms of psychological maltreatment may be used to continue control over their families even when violence may not be imminent.

Enhanced self-monitoring using the progression of violence may lead to an increased understanding and awareness of cues leading up to violent events. Learning to recognize signs of escalating tension may enhance a man's ability to alter the course of events should he choose to do so. This understanding and awareness may also help men identify critical moments in situations where the group program might help them develop alternative, nonabusive behavior.

Training in self-monitoring is often required if men are to gain a greater understanding of their own behavior and how to change it. Groups teach men to identify four categories of cues (situational, cognitive, emotional, and physical) and then to use these cues to make alternative choices about abusive behavior. In examining situational cues, men attend to repetitive patterns of situations in which abuse has occurred. These can include (a) the location of abusive incidents, such as bedroom, kitchen, or in a car; (b) the time of day, such as evening, late at night; and (c) the day of the week, such as weekends more so than weekdays. Situational cues also include a consideration of other relevant aspects of the situation such as repetitive arguments (e.g., conflict about discipline of children or money). A subcategory of situational cues that we often discuss separately with men is "red-flag words." Men frequently recognize names their partners may call them or expressions their partners use that they associate with a rapid increase in arousal.

Cognitive cues are mental images or internal dialogues that may precede abusive behavior. For example, some men find that they mentally rehearse an abusive incident prior to its occurrence. Others find themselves perseverating about an issue, for example, suspicions about a partner's infidelity. Some men identify self-talk that reflects underlying assumptions about their partners preceding abusive incidents, such as "she's trying to humiliate me" or "she doesn't care about me at all."

Group intervention should encourage men to become aware of repetitive cognitive cues and to use this awareness to change their behavior. One focus of intervention is changing the cognitions themselves, which will be discussed below in the section on cognitive restructuring.

Emotional cues refers to men's awareness of how they feel prior to abusive incidents. In early stages of safety planning, the emotion men are most aware of is anger, and the key for safety planning is the monitoring of this emotional state and using it to cue a plan for avoiding violence. Later in the intervention process, men often become aware of other feeling states that may "underlie" their anger. Often, awareness of situational cues may enhance identification of emotions. For example, one man in a group readily identified that abuse often occurred during arguments about money. In exploring this cue, he recognized, with the help of the group, that he felt inadequate and hurt during these discussions. Recognizing this emotional state may lead to the use of alternative, nonabusive behaviors for meeting his emotional needs in this situation. Emotional awareness as an intervention technique is further discussed later in this chapter.

Men most readily identify physiological cues linked to arousal. Most men can identify some physical sensations or behaviors that correspond to their most escalated states, for example, clenching fists, elevated heart rate or body temperature, tightness in their head or shoulders, to name a few. Others notice pacing, finger pointing, or speaking in a louder voice. These physical sensations may become the cues for interrupting an increasing escalation and for reducing arousal.

We have focused on the monitoring of cues that precede violent events because they often become the points for change. We also see as important, however, monitoring of the violence and the events that follow it. This is particularly true when trying to enhance men's understanding of the costs and benefits of their abusive behavior.

Techniques for teaching awareness. Arousal may be more readily interrupted when the cues are identified at earlier points in the chain of events. Weekly logs (Pence, 1989; Purdy & Nickle, 1981; Sonkin & Durphy, 1985) foster development of awareness and promote use of self-monitoring throughout intervention. Logs require men to describe situations during the week in which they behaved abusively or in which they might have become abusive if they had not chosen to act in an alternative way. Completion of the log requires men to specify their situational cues, to specify their actual behavior in the situation, and to formulate alternatives. The log also is a tool for organizing group time and for reducing time needed in group to practice alternative behaviors.

Edleson (1984a) took the log one step farther by requiring group members to draw a chain of events that graphically displayed the cues prior to, during, and following situations that were difficult for the man. These "chains" then became the focus of group discussion, exercises, and change efforts.

In discussing chains of events with clients, the implication that violent behavior is caused by external stimuli or provocations needs to be avoided. Men frequently describe their violent behavior as occurring during a period when they are "out of control." They often claim to be unaware of the functional implications of their violent behavior, such as to coerce cooperation from their partners. A critical element of treatment is helping men take more personal responsibility for their behavior and teaching them to use skills that will enable maintenance of nonviolence.

LEARNING ALTERNATIVE NONABUSIVE BEHAVIORS

There are a variety of alternative behaviors that are often taught during group sessions. These start with the development of personal safety plans that include a variety of behavioral, cognitive, and stress-reduction procedures.

Personal safety plans. Because the goal of women's safety is fore-most in working with men who batter, planning for safety takes place early in intervention and is often formalized into a contract, or agreement, to be nonviolent. These contracts include identification of cues and a plan for alternative action when the man recognizes these cues. In the earliest stages of intervention, the alternative behavior generally specified is time-out and an agreement to reach out to a hot line or someone else who will be supportive. The plans include specification of the arousal-reduction techniques to be used during the time-out. As the group progresses, men refine these agreements throughout the intervention process, as they gain more insight into cues, develop more alternative skills, and expand their definitions of what constitutes abusive behavior.

Time-out. This term has often been used in behavioral parent training programs. When used with men who batter, it refers to the ability of a man to identify a situation as one that is escalating closer to violence and to *temporarily* withdraw himself from the situation to de-escalate himself and prepare to use alternative, more respectful skills to resolve the conflict with his partner.

Men can use time-out to short-circuit the pattern of arousal that might lead to abusive behavior. Time-out generally means that men inform their partners they are becoming negatively aroused and that they need to leave the situation. The time-out procedure encourages men to leave the house and return at some later point to resolve the conflict, generally in about one hour. Time-outs give men the time to use or rehearse some of the techniques discussed below, such as arousal reduction, alteration of self-talk, problem solving solutions to the conflict, or reaching out for support from others.

Men may misuse time-out by leaving to avoid arguments with no intention of returning later to resolve the difficulties. Sometimes women perceive that their partners are using time-out inappropriately and will try stop men from leaving, through verbal or even physical restraint. Such action may greatly increase the probability of physical abuse and endanger the woman. These problems raise the need for communication with the partner regarding the time-out procedure. The time-out procedure should be explained to the man's partner and, where possible, the couple should together discuss the use of the technique.

Management of arousal. Each of the four types of cues discussed above (situational, physical, emotional, and cognitive) lends itself to specific arousal-reduction/mood-management strategies. For example, particular situations may be "managed" by the man if he carefully attends to high risk cues that commonly occur in such situations. Rosenbaum and Maiuro (1989) apply the stimulus control technique to include a focus on the characteristics of arguments that precede aggression. They note that men often identify standing up as a cue that they will act abusively toward their partners. Men are instructed to remain seated during conflictual discussions and to take a time-out if they stand up. Prolonged arguments also often precede abusive incidents. The group instructs men on setting time limits to arguments and keeping the discussions limited to single topics. Deviations from these guidelines may signal the need for time-out.

Groups often focus on teaching men a variety of methods for reducing physical arousal. Formal relaxation techniques include progressive relaxation, meditation, cue-controlled relaxation, deep breathing, autogenic relaxation, applied relaxation, and imagery-based relaxation (Woolfolk & Lehrer, 1984). With the wide proliferation and popularization of relaxation techniques, it is manageable to have men sample various types of relaxation and find one that best fits their needs. Audiotapes and self-help guides are widely available for this purpose (see for example, Girdano & Everly, 1986).

Men often prefer naturalistic techniques for arousal reduction (Rosenbaum & Maiuro, 1989), such as taking a walk, listening to soothing music, or doing some form of noncompetitive physical exercise like a bike ride. Sometimes psychopharmacological help is necessary for enhancing arousal reduction (Rosenbaum & Maiuro, 1989).

Some have suggested that tension may be reduced by aggressive, physically cathartic activities such as hitting a wall or a punching bag. This strategy, however, may not actually relieve arousal as these aggressive activities may actually increase aggressive behavior (Bandura, 1973). For this reason, noncompetitive physical exercise is probably a better option for clients who appear to require an active form of release of physical tension.

Emotional awareness. Male sex role socialization encourages men to devalue and suppress their emotions. Because anger is a more socially acceptable emotion, men learn to over-label their negative affectivity as anger, a process Gondolf (1985) refers to as the "emotional funnel." Group intervention includes training for men on how to identify other emotions. One exercise we have used in groups is to give men a "feeling chart" that lists hundreds of emotions and ask them to identify how they are feeling. Because initially men tend to identify themselves as "OK" or "fine," this is not always an easy task. Sometimes group members are asked to identify the last time they felt a negative emotion other than anger and then describe that situation.

Groups also teach men to identify other emotions that "underlie" their anger. The metaphor of anger as "secondary" emotion (McKay, Rogers, & McKay, 1989) can be used to encourage men to identify feelings other than anger. For example, a man in a recent group described himself as "pissed off" because his partner criticized how much money he was spending. In searching for the "primary emotion" beneath the anger, the group helped him to identify that he felt insecure and inadequate during the conflict, because he believed he was not making enough money and he feared his partner would leave him because of this. When these primary emotions are identified, men may be able to choose alternative behaviors to meet their emotional needs. Techniques like reaching out for support and assertive expression of feelings, discussed below, also help men to meet their emotional needs without aggression.

Cognitive restructuring. Cognitive restructuring techniques teach individuals to analyze and modify maladaptive thinking patterns. In application with groups for men who batter, Adams (1989) believes the critical aspect of internal dialogues of men who batter is that their partner's behavior is construed in such a way that justification or permission is given for abusive behavior. Edleson (1984a) has also argued that men's cognitions often lack empathy for their partners' situation.

The ecological framework is also helpful in identifying common cultural beliefs, which are taught and reinforced by society. As Adams (1989) points out, men's self-talk often reflects implicit sexist assumptions and usually has distinctly negative themes that reflect a desire to devalue and denigrate their partners rather than to respect them. Many men who batter (as well as those who do not) often believe they are entitled to control their partners' behavior. This belief may lead to confrontations over a variety of issues from finances to child care, from sex to choice of friends. Men who batter often justify their violence in terms of their entitlement to control of their partners' behavior. This belief is often reinforced by a man's social network and cultural messages. Men with rigid sex role expectations may also justify their abuse by pointing to their partners' failure to live up to those expectations.

Many men attribute their violent behavior to their inability to control their tempers: "I have a temper. My father had one. She's got to live with it" or "I don't know what got into me, I just lost control. When I see red, I do crazy things." This belief that they are not responsible for their emotions or the behaviors that result from them serves to justify their violent behavior and increases the probability of use of violence. This belief, too, is strongly reinforced in socialization of boys and men.

Men who batter may also externalize the blame for their behavior onto their partners. "If only she would know when to stop nagging at me." "If she would just take better care of the house." One often hears these types of statements from men who batter in order to justify their violence toward their partners. He sees her as the cause of his behavior. Similarly, men often blame alcohol or their childhood for their current violent behavior. The belief that past or current outside events or persons control one's behavior interferes with the development of nonviolent behavior in several ways. First, it interferes with motivation; he cannot change if he is not able to do the changing. Second, it shifts his emphasis to changing his partner's behavior rather than his own.

Beck (1976) outlines faulty thinking styles and Ellis (1970) outlines irrational beliefs that interfere with individuals' abilities to effectively handle difficult situations. These thinking patterns may, at some point, contribute to a man's use of violence (Edleson, 1984a).

For instance, arbitrary inference—drawing a conclusion when evidence is lacking or to the contrary—is often evident when jealous thoughts are aroused. In such cases, a partner's actual behavior, if it provides no justification for jealousy, may be completely ignored. Or an incident may be magnified beyond reality. For example, if a spouse talks to a male neighbor, this may lead to a belief that she is having an affair with that neighbor. In addition, dichotomous reasoning—an oversimplified perception of events as good or bad, right or wrong—plays an important role in a man's thinking about his partner's behavior and how he thinks she should behave. Conflicts over the possibility that a woman might work outside the home often represent a confrontation with a man's dichotomous reasoning about what a wife should or should not do. Labeling often reflects sexist assumptions. A man may label his partner's requests for help as nagging or her complaints about his behavior as being "bitchy."

In addition to correcting cognitive distortions, cognitive restructuring involves training men to generate new, adaptive internal dialogues that can promote nonviolence (Meichenbaum, 1977; Novaco, 1975). Men learn to generate coping self-statements that may lower arousal or encourage alternative behaviors in a high risk situation. Several group activities promote the development of cognitive skills. As mentioned, men monitor themselves weekly through the use of logs, which, among other things, ask them to be aware of their self-talk. Discussion of these situations elicits this self-talk from the men. Often, the group helps men to identify underlying irrational beliefs and faulty assumptions of their dialogues. Through practice, and support from the group, these irrational thinking styles or faulty beliefs are challenged and suggestions are made for alternative appraisals. Men then generate self-instructions for using nonviolent coping behavior. This process is supported by the use of handouts explaining self-talk and examples of "canned" self-talk men can use to help themselves cope in problematic situations.

Assertiveness and conflict resolution. Men who batter are often limited in their ability to resolve conflicts with others in an assertive manner. More often, they will act passively or aggressively (Rosenbaum & O'Leary, 1981b). An important component of group treatment for men who batter therefore involves teaching the men new interpersonal skills for conflict resolution. Applying skills training procedures with men who batter requires that a specific set of skills be identified and then taught to men, using situations that are personally relevant to them. Training in nonviolent conflict resolution often focuses on the man's ability to identify and state clearly the parameters of a problem situation, identify and express his own feelings about what is happening, identify and state his partner's point of view, offer solutions from which both he and his partner will benefit, and negotiate a final compromise.

Training often begins by identifying interpersonal situations in which the man has experienced difficulties. The logs men are assigned to keep may form the basis for identifying these situations within the group. The situations are analyzed for a critical moment, that is, the point in an interaction when the man may have acted differently to alter the outcome of the interaction. Various ways of achieving a more positive outcome are then explored in the group. After sifting through the alternatives, the man chooses one that is most likely to increase the chances of a positive resolution. This alternative is demonstrated by the leader or a group member. After observing the modeling, the man rehearses the new skill, with someone else playing the role of his partner. Group members then offer feedback on the man's performance and he may rehearse the new skills a second time to incorporate the feedback. Skills training usually culminates with an agreement to use the new skills in an upcoming situation and report back on the effect.

CONTRIBUTING TO SOCIAL CHANGE

An ecological perspective leads the practitioner away from a myopic focus on individual change. While much of what occurs in groups for men who batter addresses the individual, these groups can also foster change in the larger social environment. There are a number of ways men become agents of change in their own environments.

Groups that embrace a social change philosophy often encourage the involvement of members in mutual self-help strategies. Self-help is a social change strategy in the sense that group members become active helpers for others with the same problem. Rather than just consuming services, they commit themselves to providing service for others. They thereby evidence a commitment to helping others change and contribute to the limited resources available for stopping male violence against women. Being involved in helping others both demonstrates a man's personal responsibility for changing abusive behavior and deepens his commitment to nonviolence. While most psychoeducational groups have elements of self-help, the move toward greater reliance on self-help with batterers should occur in a systematic, graded fashion. During early structured group experiences, men may be encouraged to call other group members for support. As men demonstrate commitment within the group to achieving nonviolence, they may be asked to volunteer to tutor other men in the program. For example, men often have difficulty properly filling out log assignments and, rather than leaders taking time to help them, they can be paired with another member to help them with their difficulties. We have used this strategy in our groups with men with language or reading difficulties.

Outside of the structured groups, men may be involved in self-help in a number of ways. In Minneapolis, a system of self-help groups is set up for men to attend following their formal group involvement. These self-help groups are staffed by former group members who have established themselves as living a nonviolent life-style. These men go through training for group leadership and are paired with a professional consultant to carry out the self-help groups. Men may also be involved in staffing hot lines and in outreach to other men in crisis.

Men may also begin to change their own social networks in a direct fashion. It is not uncommon for men to encourage others to become involved in intervention. We have had men bring their brothers, fathers, and friends into the program, because they recognize that they also have problems with abusive behavior. Men may also become more supportive of their female friends and family members who are experiencing abuse at the hands of other men. Rather than contributing to the woman's isolation or self-blame, they may give clear messages about the abuse being her partner's responsibility.

Outside of direct service roles, group members may be involved in more public social change efforts when they evidence skill, commitment, and a violence-free life-style over a prolonged period of time. These public efforts may include public speaking and radio and television appearances to promote men's responsibility for ending their violence against women and children. They may participate in demonstrations or rallies. Men who have demonstrated success in leading a nonviolent life-style may be encouraged to participate in BrotherPeace activities. BrotherPeace is a national movement of men who are committed to ending male violence against women.

Men's involvement in changing societal support for men's violence may also include involvement in a spectrum of activities that are not directly focused on violence per se. The groups encourage men to challenge sexist attitudes and behaviors in their own relationships and then to extend this challenge to the men around them. Men may partake in formal and informal activities that promote changes in negative sex role socialization. Some men who have gone through batterers' programs have gotten involved in efforts to support positive fathering. Others have joined ongoing support groups.

It is important to raise a note of caution in these suggestions for the involvement of men who batter in social change efforts. There are unfortunate incidents of men who have become involved in such efforts who later prove to be continuing their abuse of their partners. Some men may be using their involvement in a manipulative manner, to convince their partners to return to them. Some may even use the involvement as a form of psychological maltreatment. His "public" image as a man committed to ending violence against women may be a purposeful contrast to his "private" abuse of his partner, increasing her sense of helplessness and isolation.

The risks of involvement of men who batter in social change cannot be taken lightly. When the goals of intervention expand to include changes beyond individual cessation of physical abuse, however, it becomes clear that there is a false dichotomy between batterers and other men, between helper and client. All men share responsibility for changing male violence against women. Every man must address the abuse in his own life, how he may use or benefit from male privilege, and how he contributes to a social environment that supports the social conditions that promote and support the inequality of women. Intervention for men who batter focuses on changing those men who most overtly or dramatically abuse their partners. The challenge we make to men who batter to change themselves must be extended to other men as well as to ourselves.

❏ Implementation Issues

We have not specified a specific length or format for the group approach described above. As discussed earlier, programs vary in terms of length, whether they are open or closed, and their degree of structure. The approach we have described can be flexibly implemented in a number of different formats to best fit local conditions. For example, at one program in which one of us is involved, Sarah's Inn Program for Men, in Oak Park, Illinois, the program begins with an intensive one-day workshop that orients men to the approach to nonviolence they will learn. These workshops meet once every 6 weeks and, following the workshop, the men join an ongoing group that meets once a week. New members are therefore integrated into ongoing groups once every 6 weeks. This format allows for new men to be added but makes the process of adding new men predictable and manageable for existing group members.

In the Sarah's Inn program, men are required to attend 18 sessions to fulfill their preliminary contracts. Presentations of basic material are repeated in a 9-week cycle, therefore men hear most key presentations at least twice. The group begins with an educational presentation given to a large group, sometimes as many as 25 men. Then the group is divided into two small groups, which have consistent membership each week. During this time, men discuss their issues and application of the approach in a smaller group, allowing for more individualized application, support, and confrontation. Some men request to stay on following their 18-week commitment, and many men are given the feedback that they have not fully completed their work within the 18-week period and it is recommended to them that they stay on for a longer period. This recommendation is forwarded to the court if they have a court mandate to attend the program and is also shared with their partners.

Similar content can be covered in other ways. At the Domestic Abuse Project in Minneapolis, for example, a closed group structure is used. Following orientation, screening, and intake sessions, men join a closed-ended 20-session group, which meets twice per week for 10 weeks. The groups of 8 to 12 men meet with one or two co-leaders. One session each week is devoted to lectures, videotapes, or demonstrations. On these nights, several groups are combined for the presentation and then divide up into the small groups for processing. On alternate nights, the small groups meet separately for the entire session. These sessions are devoted to personal issues and applications of the educational material.

In each of the programs described above, a strong emphasis is placed on completion of homework between group sessions, including completion of logs, most violent incident reports, and self-evaluations.

□ ## Evaluations of Group Intervention

OUTCOME STUDIES

Research on treatment groups for men who batter may help to determine whether woman abuse can be prevented through such intervention. Ethical practice requires a level of accountability that determines the usefulness of diverting scarce resources toward intervention with men rather than toward additional services for battered women and their children.

A number of methodological concerns must be addressed in evaluating intervention with men who batter, including definitions of abuse, sources of data, and follow-up periods. Programs differ in their definition of successful outcome (Edleson, 1990; Sonkin, 1988). Available research reflects these differences. Some studies consider reduced incidents of violent behavior a success, while others set complete cessation of violence as the criteria for success. Viewing reduction of violence as success is questionable as reduced incidences may not end the terror that battered women feel (Hart, 1988) and even so-called minor incidents of violence like slapping, pushing, and shoving may result in physical injury (Rosenbaum, 1988). Some studies report success based on ending severe violence while others include threats of violence and psychological maltreatment in determining outcome.

When comparing outcome studies, these factors must be weighed. Studies that employ success criterion of zero violence at follow-up and that use the most inclusive definitions of violence (i.e., focus beyond physical abuse) provide the highest level of program accountability as well as the greatest validity in determining whether men have changed their abusive behavior.

Several studies depend only on male self-report, which is problematic considering the evidence that suggests that men may report less violence than their partners (Edleson & Brygger, 1986; Jouriles & O'Leary, 1985; Szinovacz, 1983). Others report police arrest data; however, these data also underreport incidence, as can be seen by comparison of the police reports and women's self-reports where both have been obtained (e.g., Dutton, 1986). Most confidence can be placed in those studies using women's reports or combined male-female reports.

The studies reviewed employed follow-up periods ranging from a few weeks to several years. Most confidence can be placed in studies with lengthier follow-up periods, as men who batter may give up their abuse for a short time following intervention but later reoffend.

The percentage of program participants actually contacted for follow-up studies presents another critical evaluation issue. Some studies reach only a small percentage of participants, while others fail to report at all how many participants were actually reached. Nonparticipants in follow-up are probably more likely to be abusive (DeMaris & Jackson, 1987), and therefore success rates based on program completers may be inflated. While lengthier follow-up periods may increase the validity of success reports, the number of participants contacted usually decreases with longer follow-up.

Table 4.1 presents a synopsis of evaluations of group treatment of men who batter. Taken as a whole, the studies that have been done to date indicate that the majority of men stop their physically abusive behavior for some period of time subsequent to intervention.

Table 4.1 Outcome Studies

Study Elements	Purdy & Nickle (1981)	Halpern (1984)	Abusers Groups Edleson et al. (1985)	Hawkins & Beauvais (1985)	Dutton (1986)
N	170	70	9	106	100
Sample characteristics	3% court referred	14% court referred	0% court referred	31 years, 46% white 72% court referred	34 years, 100% court referred
Follow-up time	6 months	3 to 24 months	7 to 21 weeks	6 months	6 months to 3 years
Data collection	interviews	CTS	CTS multiple baseline	SCL-90, interview	CTS, police records
Approach	cognitive-behavioral	cognitive-behavioral	cognitive-behavioral	cognitive-behavioral	cognitive-behavioral
Number of sessions	7.8 sessions average	32	12	1 to 6 group, 6 couple and individual	16; 3 optional couples sessions
Success rate (stopped physical abuse)	59% (self-report)	85% (self-report)	77% (self-report)	NA	84% (victim report) 96% (police report)
Comparison (stopped physical abuse)	NA	noncompleters 82% (self-report)	NA	NA	untreated 40% (police report)
Statistical comparison	NA	NA	NA	NA	completers > untreated
Other outcomes/comments	follow-up procedures not reported; 14% not verbally abusive	women's reports used for some of the reports	multiple baseline showed significant reduction in violence	decrease in police calls; desirable changes on most SCL scales for completers	success rates based on severe violence

Table 4.1 Continued

		Abusers Groups			
	Hamberger & Hastings (1986)	Rosenbaum (1986)	Waldo (1986)	DeMaris & Jackson (1987)	Douglas & Perrin (1987)
N	71	12	23	53	20
Sample characteristics	NR	25.5 years, most self-referred, via shelter	27 years, 100% U.S. military in Japan	31% court	33.4 years, 35% white, 100% court referred
Follow-up time	1 year	6 months to 2 years	1 to 3 months	1 year	average 6.1 months
Data collection	CTS	telephone interviews	frequency of abusive incidents: 5 communication scales and 1 relationship scale	CTS, mail survey	police records, interview
Approach	cognitive-behavioral	psycho-educational	cognitive, modeling, behavioral	cognitive-behavioral	unspecified
Number of sessions	12			court: 12 voluntary: open-end group	
Success rate (stopped physical abuse)	72%[a]	88.8% (self-report)	reduced from average of 1.7 pre/post incidents to .29 incidents at follow-up	65% (self-report)	85% (police report) 80% (self-report)
Comparison (stopped physical abuse)	noncompleters 47% (police report)	NA	pre to post change significant	NA	noncompleters 71% (police report)

82

	Hamberger & Hastings (1986)	Rosenbaum (1986)	Waldo (1986)	DeMaris & Jackson (1987)	Douglas & Perrin (1987)
Statistical comparison	completers > noncompleters	NA	significant pre to post change on five communication scales	number of sessions not significant predictor of success	NA
Other outcomes/ comments	significant decrease in anger and depression for completers			17% follow-up response rate; no difference between court versus voluntary, high versus low attendance	improvement in depression, alcohol use, assertiveness; no change in sex attitude

continued

	Leong, Coates, & Hoskins (1987)	Shepard (1987)	Tolman et al. (1987)	Waldo (1987)	Elleson & Grusznski (1989: 1)
N Sample characteristics	67 31.6 years, 21% prior assault 100% court referred, 33% white, 80% live with spouse	77 32 years, most court referred, 99% white	48 39.8 years, 79% white	NR 100% court referred	54 29.3 years, 9% court referred, 97% white
Follow-up time	6 months	12 months average	26 months average	1 year	4.6 months average
Data collection	questionnaire computer search AMEND (Denver)	checklist—self-administered	CTS, structured interview	not reported	CTS, telephone
Approach	cognitive-behavioral, psycho-educational	cognitive-behavioral, psycho-educational	cognitive-behavioral structured	cognitive modeling behavioral	cognitive-behavioral
Number of sessions	24 or 36	12 cognitive-behavioral 12 psycho-educational	12-26	100% (source not reported)	3 orientation meetings then open end self-help, then 16 structured groups
Success rate (stopped physical abuse)	87% (police report)	69% (victim report)	53% (victim report)[b]	80% (source not reported)	67% (victim report)
Comparison (stopped physical abuse)	Noncompleters 71% (police report)	NA	NA	NA	Noncompleters 54% (victim report)
Statistical comparison	NA	NA	number of sessions not significant predictor	NA	completers > noncompleters
Other outcomes/comments	despite mandatory treatment, less than 50% were completers	41% not verbally abuse	40% not indirectly aggressive		7% severely violent (C)[b], 36% severely violent (NC)[b], ⅔ nonviolent men threaten

	Edleson & Grusznski (1989: 2)	Edleson & Grusznski (1989: 3)	Tolman & Bhosley (1989)	Edleson & Syers (1990)
N	42	84	53	92
Sample characteristics	32 years, 11% court referred, 86% white	34 years, 88% white, 7% court referred	37.2 years, 91% white	31.8 years, 74% white, 38% court referred
Follow-up time	4.6 months average	4.6 months average	12 months	6 months
Data collection	CTS, telephone	CTS, telephone	CTS, structured interview	CTS
Approach	cognitive-behavioral	cognitive-behavioral	cognitive-behavioral	cognitive-behavioral content three structures: I, Educational; II, Self-Help; III, Combined 12 or 32
Number of sessions	32	32	26	
Success rate (stopped physical abuse)	68% (victim report)	59% (victim report)	58% (victim report)[b]	I—68%, II—46%, III—66% (80 victim report, 12 self-report)
Comparison (stopped physical abuse)	NA	noncompleters 52% (victim report) completers = noncompleters	NA	NA
Statistical comparison	NA		NA	12 = 32% I = II = III
Other outcomes / comments	14% severely violent 2/3 of non-violent men threaten	15% severe violence (C) 22% severe violence (NC) 2/3 of completers threaten	26% not indirectly aggressive	No terroristic threats: I—61% II—27% III—49%

a. One year outcome combines self, police, and victim reports.
b. Includes both completers and noncompleters.

Percentages of successful outcome ranged from 53% to 85%. This surprising convergence of successful reports on different programs, with different structures and different evaluation methods, holds promise for group intervention for men who batter.

The favorable evidence for the effectiveness of group intervention must be weighed in light of other explanatory factors and with a high degree of caution with regard to methodological shortcomings. For example, lower percentages of success tended to occur in programs with lengthier follow-up and when success was based on women's reports rather than on arrests or self-reports. The evaluation studies for the most part employ nonexperimental or quasi-experimental designs. Studies of batterers who complete treatment and those that do not serve as quasi-experimental comparisons. As examination of Table 4.1 reveals, those studies report relatively small differences in most studies and few statistically significant results. The relatively successful outcomes for men who do not complete intervention suggest that other factors contribute to cessation of abuse.

PREDICTORS OF INTERVENTION SUCCESS

A few studies attempt to determine what factors may predict successful outcome of group intervention for men who batter. DeMaris and Jackson (1987) analyzed self-reports of abuse by men mandated by court to participate in a group treatment program. They found that being separated, having alcohol problems, and not calling a counselor when at risk of abuse predicted recidivism. Tolman and Bhosley (1991) examined the effect of criminal justice involvement on success in group treatment for men who batter. The odds of successfully stopping physical abuse were increased for men who had shorter histories of abuse and who attended groups on the recommendation of the police and courts. The criminal justice system contact may have increased men's awareness of the negative consequences of abuse. Only a shorter duration of abuse prior to treatment increased the odds of successful cessation of threatening behavior. This may indicate that criminal justice system involvement is most effective in deterring behavior that is most likely to result in arrest. Hamberger and Hastings (1990) report that lower levels of substance abuse, and lower narcissism, predicted successful outcome for men who batter involved in a group treatment program. These data seem to confirm the clinical axiom that men who batter need to be treated for substance abuse problems to increase the chances for successful cessation of abuse. The finding that men with higher narcissism were more likely to remain violent following treatment suggests that empathy, lacking in those with high narcissism, may be an important mediator of abusive behavior.

❑ Summary

We have presented group treatment as the first of several intervention options from which to choose when intervening with men who batter. The use of small group treatment is widespread in North America and the effect of such programs is fairly well documented. The intervention issues and procedures discussed in this chapter should be only one part of a network of community-based efforts to intervene with men. In the next chapter, we introduce individual and couple treatment that is timed to *follow* small group efforts such as discussed in this chapter and that occur in *conjunction* with other efforts such as those discussed in Chapter 6.

5

Individual and Couple Treatment

There are a variety of opinions and a great deal of debate surrounding the use of individual and, particularly, couple treatment in cases of woman abuse. Neither individual nor couple treatment should, in our opinion, be the first or primary intervention to occur in a domestic microsystem. Rather, we suggest group treatment for men who batter, and support and education groups for battered women as the first and primary intervention of choice at this level of the ecology. Our reasons for this preference were clearly set forth in the previous chapter. But, even given this preference, the usefulness of carefully timed individual or couple counseling should not be overlooked. In this chapter, we will briefly examine individual treatment and then move to a larger discussion of the issues surrounding the cautious use of couple counseling.

❑ Individual Counseling for Men who Batter

Two of the earliest reports of individual treatment for men who today would be identified as batterers were published in the mid-1970s (Bass, 1973; Foy, Eisler, & Pinkston, 1975). These reports reflect early cognitive-behavioral interventions aimed at ending violent behavior by promoting alternative communication skills or ending violent thoughts through aversive therapy (see Eisikovits & Edleson, 1989). Since the publication of these reports, little more has been written about individual counseling as a primary intervention with men who batter.

Evidently, individual treatment has been overshadowed by the development of group programs. Our experience, however, is that most men's programs provide the option of individual counseling coinciding with group sessions. The content of individual sessions often focuses on the same material presented in group sessions (see Chapter 4) but offers more personal attention than is available to individuals in groups. In educationally oriented programs, such individual sessions have even been offered as regularly scheduled "office hours" during which any members might drop in for additional assistance (Edleson & Syers, 1990).

The major drawback of individual sessions is the loss of the group's social environment. The various forms of social support, modeling and feedback for change, and peer confrontation that take place in a group are mostly absent in individual counseling. It has also been our experience that initial accounts that deny individual responsibility for and the results of men's abusive behavior are easier to maintain when confronted only by a counselor as opposed to a group of peers—men in similar situations—who often hold each other accountable for their statements.

As a result of these drawbacks, we see individual counseling as an important but supplementary microsystem intervention. It is an intervention that may be able to support group programs but is unlikely to replace the benefits of such groups.

❏ The Cautious Use of Couple Treatment

Couple counseling in cases of woman abuse has generated more interest and controversy than individual treatment efforts. A growing number of authors are reporting clinical programs and evaluations of them. If timed carefully, couple counseling may provide an important supplement or follow-up for men (and women) who participate in groups. Couple counseling should be used only when the safety of victims can be assured. Practically, this usually occurs only when a set of specific criteria have been met and only then in certain prescribed circumstances.

In the remainder of this chapter, we will present the controversial issues surrounding the use of couple treatment, describe the criteria that should be met before bringing a couple together for counseling, and describe how such counseling might be conducted in a safe manner. We end the chapter with a review of what evidence currently exists concerning the effectiveness of couple counseling in cases of woman abuse.

Much of the controversy surrounding the use of couple treatment concerns the view one holds about violent events and the role of both the man and the woman in such events. These diverse views may primarily be grouped according to three themes: (a) the centrality of the relationship to violence, (b) our society's focus on family preservation, and (c) the structure of couple treatment.

RELATIONSHIP AND VIOLENCE

The degree of centrality accorded relationship factors is a pivotal issue in the debate over whether and when to use couple counseling in cases of woman abuse (see Edleson, 1984b). Some family-oriented practitioners see violence between a related man and woman as "by definition an interpersonal transaction" and go on to "reject labels 'abuser' and 'victim,' believing that neither partner has an exclusive right to either term" (Neidig, 1984, pp. 469-470). Such positions reflect what is so often the focal point in the controversy surrounding the use of couple treatment.

To say that a man's use of violence against his intimate woman partner is an "interpersonal" or "transactional" problem is not much different than saying the rape of a woman by an acquaintance is an "interpersonal" issue in which both the male rapist and the female victim somehow share responsibility for the event. This implies that the victim is to blame for the perpetrator's behavior.

In addition, using the language of "transactions," "violent relationships," or "battering system" submerges the fact that violence, especially severe violence, is most often perpetrated by a husband against a wife and lessens the personal accountability of the violent individual (Bograd, 1984). To speak in the language of "transactions" minimizes the fact that a crime has been committed.

The language of mutual responsibility for violence tends to reinforce the long-held beliefs that violence by a man toward his wife is different than and thus exempt from current laws concerning behavior toward others. This attitude reduces a woman's basic rights when she enters an intimate relationship with a man. Such attitudes are contrary to emerging views of women's basic human rights as discussed in Chapter 2.

Few would disagree that many of the relationships in which violence occurs may not be models of healthy communication. Some couple therapists, however, have viewed violence as only one symptom of an underlying communication dysfunction in the relationship (see, for example, Lane & Russell, 1989). A danger is that the importance of violence will be minimized, the physical violence will be made equal to verbal abuse problems being experienced (Bograd, 1984), and the influential ecological factors such as historical precedents and macrosystem beliefs will be ignored.

FAMILY PRESERVATION

Societal values and beliefs about relationships and their importance also play a major role in the controversy over the use of couple treatment. Some couple and couple group therapy programs seek to repair relationships in addition to ending violence between the man and woman. This is consistent with dominant macrosystem values that form the foundation of family therapy. These values focus priority on maintaining and enhancing nuclear families. Evidence of such dominant values can be seen in the dramatic growth of "family preservation" programs during the 1980s (see Miller & Whittaker, 1988; Nelson, Landsman, & Deutelbaum, 1990).

There is consensus in the field that an examination of violence rates sometime following the end of treatment should be the central criteria for judging a program's success. There is, however, a great deal of controversy over whether or not reuniting a couple should be a desired outcome goal in cases of woman abuse. The preference to see couples reunited is sometimes expressed in subtle ways. For example, Neidig, Friedman, and Collins (1985) collect and report ratings by couples on the Dyadic Adjustment Scale, an indicator of couple relationship adjustment. They present improvement in couple adjustment scores as a desirable outcome of their treatment program.

Many couple interventions do not explicitly aim to repair relationships. The use of marital satisfaction ratings and data on both improved communication or decreased arguments indicates, however, that such improvements have been raised to a criterion of success. This raises a serious question: How can a treatment program that uses improved relationships as an indicator of success also see as successful the dissolution of the relationship to provide greater safety to victims? Many have argued that whether or not the couple remains together or is reunited following violence is irrelevant to the success of woman abuse interventions. In some cases, the couple may safely reunite and rebuild their relationship. In other cases, it may be necessary to help the couple separate and build new lives independent of each other.

STRUCTURE OF COUPLE TREATMENT

The very structure of couple treatment has also been the focus of attention (Bograd, 1984). Several major points have been raised when criticizing the structure of couple treatment. These include the degree to which a woman is safe to speak openly in treatment, the implicit message present when a couple is brought together for treatment, the neutrality between man and woman that is traditionally sought by couple therapists, and the likelihood that the therapist will work more intensively with a woman who is eager to change rather than a man who is reluctant to do so (see Bograd, 1984).

The first point is whether a woman's safety can be assured in couple treatment. Some therapists have stated that this can be achieved by an agreement at the outset that no violence will be used while the couple is in treatment (Rabin, Sens, & Rosenthal, 1982). Our experience is, however, that such an agreement is frequently violated and does not ensure a woman's safety. An analogy we have found useful to consider is the one in which a couple is sitting talking to their counselor. The man, unknown to the therapist, waved a gun at his wife before they left home and threatened to use it against her if she said anything in couple counseling that might put him in a negative light. The man then sat through the therapy session, mostly quiet, while carefully monitoring his wife's statements. His woman partner, knowing the possible consequences of honest responses, carefully chooses her words and avoids expressing the many feelings she is experiencing.

We would argue that the above scenario of hidden threats is a reality for many battered women who enter couple counseling as their first and primary form of treatment. This is especially true in situations where the counselor only meets with the couple as a "system" and not individually. In such cases, it is clearly unsafe for a woman to openly express feelings of fear, rage, and anger or to describe the reality of her everyday life. This structure may create a dangerous situation for the woman if she takes a risk and is honest with the couple's counselor.

Another point of contention with couple treatment concerns the implicit message evident when a couple is immediately brought together in conjoint treatment. The message seems to stress the importance of working on the microsystem interactions that occur between the man and woman (Libow, Raskin, & Caust, 1982). The message is not that work with the man as an individual or his other microsystems is important. This may send the message that both the man and the woman share responsibility for the violence, which would be especially true if the language of "transactions" were applied.

The controversy here is, in part, over whether or not a victim should take any responsibility for another's violent behavior. It is also about whether or not couple counseling in cases of woman abuse, by its very structure, reinforces macrosystem norms that often shift responsibility for violence from male perpetrators to women against whom the violence has been committed.

Two additional concerns about the structure of couple treatment are often raised. First, most couple therapists are trained to remain neutral in disputes between the couples they are counseling so that they may form therapeutic alliances with both members of the couple. This neutrality may give a message of equal responsibility between the man and woman for violent incidents. In addition, systemic intervention within couple relationships often calls on counselors to work with the part of the system that is most open to change (Bograd, 1984). As a result of male and female socialization in many societies, women are most often the ones who are most concerned about the family and more willing to adapt to others' desires to nurture and maintain it. Therefore the counselor may find him- or herself working more with the woman to make changes in her part of the system with the hope that it will have an effect on the reluctant male partner. Here again, responsibility for change is shifted from the man who perpetrates the violence to the victim of the abuse, thus reinforcing the long-held societal beliefs mentioned so often in this book.

SUMMARY

A couple's "interpersonal transactions" may be only one small part of the problem. We do not see these transactions as the sole source of the violence nor do we believe they should necessarily be the central target of efforts to stop the violence. It is our view that the goal of intervention should be to end violence and should not be judged on whether or not a relationship survives that violence. The danger in doing otherwise is to risk achieving family preservation at the cost of continuing violence.

Responsible Use of Couple Treatment

By this point, one might expect that we would now argue that under no circumstances should couple treatment be selected for use in cases of woman abuse. We believe, however, that, even considering the above concerns, there is a time and place for couple intervention. We view couple treatment as appropriate when certain criteria have been met and then only in certain circumstances. The timing of when such procedures are used is of the utmost importance. Also critical is that couple counseling commence only when each partner has expressed an interest in reuniting and/or rebuilding their relationship. The counselor must be sensitive to the pervasive effects of the abuse and take special precautions to ameliorate its effects in counseling.

CRITERIA FOR USING COUPLE TREATMENT

There are specific criteria one must consider before agreeing to conduct couple counseling. These criteria concern the man's current attitudes and behavior, the woman's perception of her safety, and both partners' desire to remain together.

Once a man has made a commitment to becoming nonabusive, then couples work may be an important component of service. This commitment may be demonstrated in several ways. He will have participated in group treatment for a period of at least several months during which he will have been successful in remaining nonviolent and will not have inflicted psychological maltreatment on his partner.

A significant amount of time prior to the start of couple counseling is necessary. Our experience is that men may readily suppress overtly abusive behavior at the outset of treatment, especially if they believe that such suppression will lessen the consequences of their abusive behavior. The choice of the word *suppress* is meant to imply that a man's change in behavior is only temporary and will later reemerge once he is confident that he has avoided the immediate negative consequences of it. To engage in couples work, he will also demonstrate an understanding that his psychological maltreatment of his partner is of concern and will be committed to changing that behavior as well. An identifiable pattern of ongoing maltreatment would make couples work contraindicated.

The reader may wonder at this point what role couples work has in helping men become nonabusive if cessation of abuse is a prerequisite for participation. In one sense, the answer is that it does not play a role per se in the cessation of abuse. As discussed above, violence is not seen as an interactional issue. Couples counseling, however, may be critical to the positive functioning of a relationship destroyed by the abuse. Much like longer group treatment, it can help consolidate a man's changing behavior and help him develop an increasing competence in becoming a supportive partner rather than an abusive one.

Couples counseling also offers specific benefits to battered women who have chosen to rebuild their relationships. It may provide a safe forum for helping her to express feelings. Ideally, she has begun to process these feelings in a supportive environment prior to joint counseling. Bancovics and Kittel (1983) suggest prerequisites for women's participation in couples work. These include the following: (a) She does not believe she deserves his abusive behavior nor does she feel she can control it; (b) she has developed an effective safety plan and can assess when she needs to use such a plan to protect herself and her children; and (c) she has available to her and will use various resources for protection. The fulfillment of these prerequisites limits the potential dangers of couples work. If a woman has resolved any feelings of self-blame she may have had, she will not be as vulnerable to explicit or implicit messages that she must change for the abuse to stop. Because couples work is stressful and the risk of repeat violence is always present, it is important that she be prepared to protect herself in the event that her partner continues to abuse her while in couples treatment. If these conditions are not met, the risk of harm resulting from couples treatment may be increased.

STEPS IN COUPLES TREATMENT

Couples work progresses in a series of steps, in which successful completion of a step is a prerequisite for moving further in the work. These steps include addressing the abuse, rebuilding relationship commitment, building relationship skills, and resolving ongoing conflicts.

> *Open expression of the resentment that abusive behavior has engendered may facilitate a battered woman's ability to heal.*

Addressing the abuse. The first step in doing couples work is to address directly the impact the abuse has had in the relationship. This is very often the element missed in traditional couples work. In behavioral marital therapy, for example, Stuart (1980) argues convincingly that treatment should start with a positive induction rather than with a review of complaints and negative content. Our view, however, is that the impact of abuse is generally so severe that it must be dealt with explicitly at the outset of couples work. Open expression of the resentment that abusive behavior has engendered may facilitate a battered woman's ability to heal. Very often, women feel a great deal of pentup rage and need a supportive environment in which to express it. Couples work needs to begin with an acknowledgment and validation of these feelings before other couple goals can be attained.

One method for addressing these issues is through structured sessions, set explicitly with the goal of her sharing with her partner her reactions to the abuse. Frequently, this process takes place over the course of several sessions. First, the woman shares the abuse she has experienced. She describes to her partner in detail her recollection of abusive incidents, how she has been hurt by the abuse, physically and emotionally, and how she currently feels about the abuse.

A man's task in these sessions is to listen carefully and hopefully with empathy, responding only with statements that indicate how he understands what she is saying. The practitioner instructs him not to rebut statements or attempt to defend himself. Ideally, he has practiced this skill of reflective listening earlier in his men's group experience. In a sense, the couples session offers a difficult mastery task: He must listen effectively to very painful material, which he is likely to want to defend himself against. The benefits of this exercise therefore extend beyond providing expression of the abused woman's feelings. It can provide a mechanism for evaluating his ability to tolerate her expression of negative affect and his level of denial. Asking him to focus on empathic listening fosters a critical relationship skill that will be addressed in further steps of the couples work.

The structure of these sessions prevents them from turning into conflicts. He may be upset by what he hears, but open conflict is purposefully suppressed in session. The need to assess safety and plan for it is paramount, however. Both partners must be warned about the potential for negative feelings. Both should review their safety plans, preferably individually. Some individual processing time is also desirable, following the conjoint portion of the session, to review the session and its impact on each partner and to check on safety concerns.

At times, these sessions must be stopped because men become escalated and cannot tolerate the content. This highlights the need for him to have successfully demonstrated an ability to deal with his aggressive behavior prior to couples work. While these procedures are particularly stressful, we do not believe the material is qualitatively different than the kind of conflictual material that comes up in the course of other couples work. If he is able to successfully de-escalate, the session may begin again, or another session may be held later.

Some couples do not progress beyond this step. At times, a woman judges by her partner's inappropriate reactions that he is not ready to begin couples work safely. She discovers he is not ready to fully hear her pain. At this point, it may be necessary for both parties to reconsider their desire to remain together.

While successful completion of these structured sessions may begin the healing process, the need to deal with the impact of abuse on the relationship is ongoing. The fear, mistrust, rage, and other barriers to intimacy that the victim feels must be readdressed and processed throughout couples treatment.

Increasing positive behavior. The second primary goal of couples work is to instigate increases in positive behavior. The use of exercises to instigate such increases may have short-term but positive effects. Members of the couple learn to pay attention to the quality of relationship, to identify problem areas where they exist, and to learn how to please their partners in effective ways (Jacobson & Holtzworth-Munroe, 1986). An increase in positive behavior when accompanied by a cessation of abusive behavior will also foster a recommitment to the relationship, if it is possible.

One exercise we have used to instigate positive behavior is the Caring Days exercise (Stuart, 1980). The Caring Days exercise or a similar one is often used as a first step in social learning approaches to marital counseling. The technique asks each person to identify specific positive behaviors the other partner could do to show they care. The behaviors chosen should be small (e.g., call during the day to say hello, ask how the partner's day has been), nonconflictual, and positively stated (e.g., "compliment my appearance" rather than "stop putting down my appearance"). Each partner agrees to do several of these things each day for a week. The other partner monitors whether or not the caring behaviors are actually exhibited by her partner.

This step redirects the couples work to positive themes and has the goal of encouraging exchange of positive behavior. Prior to this exercise, these behaviors may have been recently shared only during "honeymoon" periods. Key elements of the Caring Days exercise include the "Change First" rule. Such a rule emphasizes individual responsibility and gets couples out of infinite regress in a spiral of "she (he) didn't, so I didn't." Completion of this exercise can provide important assessment data. One common pattern is for women to take responsibility for the positive behaviors while men do not do their share. He may respond with typical externalization of responsibility, as described above. An inability to complete this task with some success—that is, both partners successfully completing some caring behaviors on most days—may signal that it is not yet time to begin this work or that further confrontation is necessary.

Relationship skills. If the couple successfully completes these initial steps, they may move to building the skills necessary for a successful relationship. The emphasis in this stage is not on ongoing conflicts or difficulties but on the tools necessary for resolving such difficulties.

We draw on a cognitive-behavioral framework for teaching relationship skills to couples at this stage in the work. Such procedures have been detailed in various sources (see Gottman, Notarius, Gonso, & Markman, 1976; Jacobson & Margolin, 1979; Stuart, 1980) and are only briefly outlined here. The skills taught include receptive and expressive communication skills and problem-solving training. This content mirrors some of the skills introduced in the men's groups. The importance of receptive, empathic listening is emphasized first, with common obstacles to good listening labeled and then identified in the couple's own behavior.

Early sessions focus on each partner having a chance to get the "floor," while the other partner attempts to communicate that he or she has understood the content and validated the feelings of the other. Expressive skills are also introduced in early sessions. Partners learn to make "I statements" and to avoid common communication pitfalls. Problem solving may be greatly enhanced by improved listening and expressive skills.

To further enhance problem solving, couples are encouraged to separate dispute resolution into two stages. In the first stage, the goal is for each partner to feel that he or she is being heard and validated. If emotions escalate during this time, it may be necessary to take a short break to allow intense feelings to subside. After the break, the couple may return to the disagreement and attempt to negotiate a solution. This break may be relatively short (15-30 minutes) or may need to be more protracted. As part of this process, couples are also taught to use both formal and informal contracts to aid in the problem-solving process. Skill training sessions may also include training in parenting, money management, and other issues.

Counselor behavior in these skill training sessions is highly active. The counselors, we hope, will model relationship skills through role-plays with each partner. As couples discuss problem areas, counselors need to be careful to quickly identify destructive relationship behaviors and suggest alternatives rapidly, modeling them if necessary. We find it helpful to give couples written materials and to suggest relevant homework assignments after each session.

We have tended to use a relatively highly structured approach in these early sessions because we believe it enhances the skill training and reduces the potential for highly emotional, destructive interaction during the couple session. We try to lower couples' expectations about solving disputes during this stage and to keep them focused on process rather than product during this time. As sessions progress to the next stage, the structure becomes looser and the content of sessions becomes more client determined.

Conflict resolution. Equipped with the skills necessary to successfully resolve relationship concerns, couples can then move on to addressing ongoing problematic issues. At this point, couples may address the ongoing points of disagreement in their relationship. Problems in disciplining the children, relationships with extended family members, and family finances may now be addressed with a diminished threat of abuse. Areas of the relationship that have been adversely affected by abuse, such as affection and intimacy, or open sharing of confidences, may also be discussed and hopefully healed.

This stage may be protracted. Throughout this stage, however, abuse-related issues tend to resurface, and previous work may need to be repeated and expanded. For instance, at any point, a woman may find herself intimidated by a gesture of her partner that she interprets as threatening. Work must be redirected away from the content being discussed and to helping the man to be empathic to his partner as they both work through the effects of his prior abuse.

OTHER ISSUES IN COUPLES WORK

As in couples counseling in other contexts, family of origin issues are likely to surface in couples work. Because of the high probability that abusive men may have experienced violence in their families of origin, the need for work in this area may be heightened. Ideally, couples come to understand what the other learned about intimacy in his or her own family, with insight from this exploration helping them to better manage their own relationship. This work requires a supportive context where both members of the couple can expose vulnerabilities, so any intensive family of origin work is generally conducted later in the course of counseling.

Frequently, it becomes clear during couples work that the relationship will not work. One or both partners are unable to make a commitment to reestablish intimacy. One particularly difficult issue is when it seems clear to the counselor that the relationship is not being reestablished in a productive manner. As in individual work with battered women, it becomes critical not to push either partner to leave or terminate the relationship. Such a stance may alienate the couple or force them out of intervention. Each partner may feel like a failure or defective for remaining in a relationship the practitioner views as hopeless or unhealthy. For example, the male partner in one couple seen in treatment began to attend sessions irregularly. His partner complained that, while he was not hitting her, he was not following through on improving the relationship. At a session that he did not attend, the female cotherapist showed her impatience and directly suggested it was time for the battered woman to think about how she could continue without being in a relationship with her husband. They both showed up at the next session angry at the counselor for suggesting it was time to break up the relationship. The couple stated their intention to leave counseling. Unfortunately, it was now too late to back off this clinical error effectively and the couple left treatment. In time, if the counselor was on target, the women might have made the decision to leave for herself and then she would have had support for getting out of the relationship.

When a couple does move toward separation or decides not to reunite, then the couples counseling may serve as a forum for conciliation. In the context of a supportive environment, the couple may make decisions about visitation, custody, division of property, and other issues. This does not imply, however, that such conciliation work should be routine with couples where there is woman abuse. In fact, we oppose such a strategy. Conciliation or mediation should, in our view, only be conducted if the prerequisites for couples work described above are met and maintained throughout the process of counseling.

❏ The Effectiveness of Couple Treatment

We have proposed that couples work can be one aspect of ecological intervention with men who batter. We do not see it as a means of stopping violence but as an intervention to improve relationships of couples who choose to stay together after the man has made a commitment to ending his abusive behavior. The model described is based exclusively on clinical experience and has not as yet been subjected to rigorous evaluation.

The goal of such couples counseling is not to end violence, but it is important to carefully monitor whether recurrence of abuse is more or less likely to occur as a result of such intervention. Increased levels of abuse occurring during couples work may indicate that the assumption that such intervention can occur with safety for the woman is incorrect. While the success of such work should not be based on couples staying together, it is necessary to know whether treated couples who do stay together are likely to achieve more respectful, egalitarian relationships than those who do not. If couples choose not to remain together as a result of counseling, but separate in a less volatile, less destructive manner, then this too would be considered successful couples intervention.

Some research does exist on the success of couple counseling as the *first and primary* method for ending abuse. It is surprising, however, given the number of advocates of this type of treatment, that very little systematic research has yet been reported on such interventions. The few evaluations that have been reported can be grouped into studies of (a) conjoint counseling and (b) multicouple group treatment. These studies provide very limited support for the effectiveness of couple treatment and raise a variety of questions that are addressed in the review below.

CONJOINT COUNSELING

Only three evaluations of conjoint couple counseling could be found in the published literature. Lindquist, Telch, and Taylor (1985) reported 6-week and 6-month follow-ups with couples receiving therapy for the man's violence. They found that 50% of the couples treated experienced at least one incident of violence during the initial 6 weeks following the program and that, at 6 months after treatment, all couples interviewed had experienced violent incidents. No comparison data were supplied for control couples.

More positive outcomes are reported by Harris (1986) and Taylor (1984). Harris (1986) evaluated a model based on Walker's (1979) proposed model of couple counseling. Couples began with several individual counseling sessions and then continued with conjoint sessions interspersed with individual ones for the remainder of treatment. The focus was primarily cognitive-behavioral, aimed at ending the man's violence and appropriately placing responsibility for the violence. Harris contacted 30 couples from 2 months to 3 years after treatment and found 73% of the couples were "successful." She does not, however, clearly define how success has been operationalized.

Taylor (1984) also adopts a primarily cognitive-behavioral approach when working with couples. His approach views (a) anger as learned and intensified by stress and intrapersonal cognitions, (b) the couple's behavior as developing into an abusive system in which both abuser and victim learn specific, complementary roles, and (c) the abusive behavior as being associated with low self-esteem, feelings of powerlessness, and inadequate problem-solving skills. Taylor takes couples through an eight-stage, skill building program that includes observing stressful cues, changing internal cognitive dialogues, and learning to express oneself more assertively and to better resolve conflicts. He briefly states that, of the 50 couples with whom he has worked, 65% reported that there had been no new violence in the 6 months following treatment. He does not state how these data were collected or who reported them to him.

Taylor is not alone in being vague about the reporters of his data. Existing studies of couple intervention have seldom stated the sources of their outcome data. Differences between the level of violence reported by men and women in the same relationship are dramatic and well documented in numerous studies of violent incident reports offered by couples (see Edleson & Brygger, 1986; Jouriles & O'Leary, 1985; Szinovacz, 1983). To simply state that couples reported they were not violent at follow-up may be misleading. Research indicates that, if the violent man is the sole reporter of violence at follow-up, the success of an intervention may be greatly inflated.

MULTICOUPLE GROUPS

The most outcome data reported to date have concerned the effectiveness of multicouple group interventions. Peter Neidig and Jeanne Deschner are the most consistent proponents of the group approach and are the only ones to have reported outcome data. Neidig's approach has been clearly described both in an article (Neidig et al., 1985) and in a book (Neidig & Friedman, 1984). Titled the Domestic Conflict Containment Program (DCCP), this approach offers a highly structured, 10-session skill building and cognitive-restructuring program to groups of couples. It is focused on eliminating violence between couples and sees abuse as a relationship issue; that is, both parties participate in abusive behavior although not always equally. Groups focus upon six steps: accepting responsibility for violence and other behaviors, contracting for change, learning safety mechanisms, understanding sequences of violence, mastering anger control, and learning to better contain interpersonal conflict.

Neidig et al. (1985) report they found the 100 or so couples with whom they worked to exhibit "typically significant positive change" on the Nowicki-Strickland Locus of Control Scale and the Dyadic Adjustment Scale (p. 204). They also report that, at 4 months after treatment, about 87% of the participants were violence free but, like Taylor, they do not state (a) who has reported the data they include in their results or (b) whether or not this figure includes the women participants who were probably not violent at the beginning of treatment.

Deschner (1984; Deschner & McNeil, 1986; Deschner, McNeil, & Moore, 1986) has also carefully detailed her programmatic approach to working with couples in groups. Deschner bases her approach on a model that combines Walker's (1979) cycle of violence and Patterson and Hops's (1972) coercion spiral. She hypothesizes that the cycle of violence goes through the following seven stages: mutual dependency, noxious event, coercive exchange, last-straw decision, primitive rage (violence), withdrawal, and repentance. Her 10-session program provides separate therapy to subgroups of men and women during the first half of each meeting and then combines the couples for the second half of each meeting to receive didactic instruction.

Deschner et al. (1986) report that 47 persons who completed training reported significantly fewer arguments, less anger, and higher relationship satisfaction. While violence decreased, the change was not statistically significant. In an 8-month follow-up of 15 couples, 8 were violence free. Five couples who participated in their program later experienced up to four "minor physical incidents such as grabbing or slapping the partner" (p. 60). Deschner considers all of these 13 couples (87%)—including the 5 in which there were "minor" incidents—to be free of battering. Deschner and McNeil (1986) state that, for 47 persons, violence decreased by only 50% and that this too was not a statistically significant change. It is unclear whether the 47 persons reported in each of the two articles are the same sample. An earlier group of 22 program participants was also reported to be "less inclined" to anger, depression, and aggression after treatment (Deschner & McNeil, 1986). In an appendix to her book, Deschner (1984) reports similar results for what appears to be the same group of 22 program participants: 12 men and 10 women. It is unclear whether reported results include nonviolent women victims as part of the success rates or whether the rates include only members of the couple who were initially identified as violent.

SUMMARY

We have argued that couple intervention in cases of woman abuse must be approached with great caution. We see it as a useful intervention when implemented at a particular time and when specific criteria have been met. We do not see it as a desired primary or first intervention within the family.

Claims and counterclaims concerning the value of such interventions are frequently voiced but few have examined the empirical evidence on effectiveness. Our review illustrates that one cannot yet make a judgment about the effectiveness of couple-based interventions in these cases. Given all the methodological shortcomings, it is clear that a great deal of additional research is needed to prove the value of couple treatment for men who batter and battered women.

As is the theme throughout this book, couple intervention should be seen as one of a variety of possible interventions with men who batter. A danger is that, due to our culture's emphasis on family preservation and the power of the psychotherapeutic treatment community (see Dobash & Dobash, 1992), we will overlook other possible points of intervention in the ecology. As the next chapter will illustrate, many alternative points of intervention in the mesosystem and exosystem that involve larger systems exist and are being successfully developed.

6

Social System Interventions

Our integrated analysis of woman abuse calls for interventions at all levels of the social ecology, not just with individuals, couples, or small groups of men. As we stated in Chapter 2, a violent man's environment is full of social institutions that indirectly affect his life and that therefore are important targets of intervention. These institutions include schools, hospitals, religious institutions, places of employment, and the criminal justice system—to name but a few.

Some of the most concerted efforts to intervene with men who batter have occurred at the institutional level. Battered women's advocates, in particular, have worked hard to change the ways in which a wide array of institutions respond to both men who batter and their victims. These efforts usually play themselves out directly in the man's life through changed responses to his violence by such diverse actors as the local police officer, minister, doctor or nurse, schoolteacher, and social worker. A man's interaction with his minister regarding violence represents one of many interactions he may have with individual representatives of larger social systems. The likelihood that this man will receive a congruent and influential message about his violent behavior will be greatly enhanced if his minister is giving a message consistent with that of the police officer, the nurse, and the neighbor. Efforts to coordinate responses of these diverse actors often take place without the man's direct knowledge but play themselves out in his and his victims' everyday lives.

❑ Prevention and Early Intervention Efforts

It would seem desirable to prevent problems from developing by starting to change the social values and models to which a man is exposed early in his development. In addition, it would also seem desirable to intervene at the first sign of trouble rather than waiting for a severe crisis to develop. Unfortunately, U.S. society tends to focus on problems once they have occurred rather than attempting to prevent their occurrence. For example, funding and social effort is increasingly devoted to those working with the most severe cases of child abuse while less severe cases are often left unattended. The same is true for woman abuse. The most severe cases receive society's attention while efforts to prevent future instances of abuse or intervene early go unfunded or underfunded.

We start this chapter by presenting several examples of preventive and early intervention efforts in educational, religious, medical, and employment settings. Unfortunately, these efforts are mostly isolated examples waiting to be replicated and adapted. Following a presentation of these isolated efforts, we will focus on a more detailed examination of the many coordinated intervention projects currently under way in criminal justice systems.

EDUCATIONAL SETTINGS

One of the most logical avenues to influencing future behavior is through contact with children and adolescents in the educational system. One such effort, reported by Levy (1984), resulted in the production of a curriculum package for 13- to 18-year-olds in Southern California. The curriculum, titled *Skills for Violence-Free Relationships,* was developed jointly with the Southern California Coalition on Battered Women and the Junior League of Los Angeles. Designed to be used in schools as well as other youth-oriented settings, the curriculum focuses on helping youth develop four major areas of knowledge and skill: (a) defining abuse, (b) understanding the myths and facts of domestic violence, (c) comprehending the social and psychological contributors to abuse, and (d) developing skills that provide alternatives to abuse, such as stress management, conflict resolution, and assertion skills. These areas are covered through a variety of brainstorming, discussion, role-play, and experiential activities. There is no fixed length or number of sessions in this curriculum. Rather, educators may tailor the materials and activities to the particular needs of the audience.

Other projects within educational and youth settings have only recently been reported. Levy's (1991) recent edited volume on dating violence contains several additional examples. In one such effort, Jones (1991) describes the introduction of material concerning woman abuse to an entire state's school-age population. The Minnesota project provided training to "400 teachers and other school personnel from 210 schools in 146 districts" (p. 261). The 400 teachers and other school personnel were trained in the delivery of a multimedia curriculum including a videotape and handouts based on the Southern California curriculum (Levy, 1984). An evaluation comparing students in classes where the curriculum was delivered with those in classes where it was not delivered revealed that knowledge about woman abuse and community resources increased significantly. Student attitudes about male and female roles in intimate relationships did not, however, change significantly (Jones, 1991).

RELIGIOUS SETTINGS

Another point of preventive intervention in North American communities is religious institutions. Teachings about appropriate behavior toward others are central to religious institutions, and clergy are often the first persons to whom troubled congregants turn. The fact that clergy frequently counsel battered women congregants was supported in a survey of North American Protestant clergy

(Alsdurf, 1985), which found 84% had counseled battered women in their congregations.

The importance of clergy in prevention and early intervention has led to a variety of efforts. These include theological discussions of domestic violence, materials produced specifically for use in congregations, and training for clergy on how to work on domestic violence within their congregations.

Fortune and Hertze (1987) and Pellauer (1983) have outlined the various roles clergy and secular counselors may play as well as the religious issues that may influence both Christian and Jewish efforts to intervene. Similarly, Spitzer (1985) has published a comprehensive historical and contemporary analysis of the Jewish laws and responses to woman abuse.

In more concrete terms, Halsey (1987) suggests a variety of activities that congregations may undertake to "break the silence" concerning abuse within their communities. These include setting up a study group, examining the various theological messages given within the daily lives of the congregation, sponsoring educational events or series for the congregation, developing closer linkages with local social services, setting up volunteer social services sponsored by the congregation, initiating new services that fill existing gaps in the community or advocating for them in the larger community, and even setting up peer support groups for victims within the congregation. To facilitate these efforts, Spitzer (1985) and others have also developed materials, including sermons on domestic violence, that can be adapted for congregational use.

MEDICAL SETTINGS

Hospital staff are also often the first to have contact with victims of abuse. A number of hospital interventions in woman abuse have been developed (Goodwin, 1985; Klingbeil, 1986; Kurz, 1987) to enhance the effectiveness of medical personnel handling these cases.

Klingbeil (1986) has described a comprehensive set of steps through which hospitals might proceed when developing interventions in woman abuse. Klingbeil has been instrumental in developing the domestic violence interventions at Harborview Medical Center in Seattle, Washington, where these steps have been implemented.

The process Klingbeil has described begins with a clear policy statement by hospital management that intervention in intrafamily violence is part of the hospital's mission. The next step is to develop a comprehensive packet of information including incidence data and statements of principles guiding intervention. This becomes the basis for the third step, developing written procedures for each department that draw upon both the policy statement and the information packet. Such procedures might include design and dissemination of brochures for patients and establishing multidisciplinary review committees. The final two steps of Klingbeil's comprehensive model include both developing linkages with other community resources and implementing an ongoing evaluation of the hospital's response.

In departments that are likely to receive numerous cases, such as emergency rooms, Klingbeil suggests an additional step of developing specific step-by-step protocols to enhance the consistency of responses. Several other authors have also suggested protocols for use in emergency rooms. For example, Campbell and Sheridan (1989) have proposed detailed assessment guidelines for nurses to apply when emergency room staff handle a case of woman abuse. Their guidelines focus on the assessment of both life- and health-threatening problems and offer possible interventions that may be implemented by nurses both within the medical system and in coordination with other systems. Hunt (1990) has also emphasized the importance of developing thorough identification and documentation procedures in medical settings.

Such changes in protocol often occur as a result of internal efforts. Particularly interesting is Kurz's (1987) description of a successful effort by a physician assistant to change the protocol in one emergency room:

> The advocate made several changes in her ED (Emergency Department). First, she developed and received approval for a file card system which all staff were to use to note the battering cases they identified. These cases would then be referred to the physician assistant or the ED social worker who was concerned about battering. The ED director put treatment of battering into the official ED manual, and also allowed the physician assistant to conduct training sessions on battering for new residents and interns. (pp. 76-77)

While these protocol changes appear small scale, Kurz (1987) found that they resulted in this emergency room being much more likely to responded positively to battered women than three others he had studied.

EMPLOYMENT SETTINGS

Employers often experience firsthand the economic costs of violence. They receive hospital billings, pay higher insurance benefits, and experience lower worker productivity as a result. Due to financial and legal necessity, employers are becoming much more active in several important areas: (a) They are attempting to internally manage health care cases of their employees; (b) they are increasing the mental health assessment and referral that is offered to employees through Employee Assistance Programs (EAPs); and (c) they are taking a more active role in educating their workers concerning such issues as sexual harassment. It would appear, given these trends, that the foundations may be in place for adding preventive intervention in domestic violence at places of employment.

Undoubtedly, EAPs serve both perpetrators and victims of abuse, but have not been effectively identified those clients.

No doubt, EAPs have been serving both perpetrators and victims of woman abuse but have not been effectively identifying those clients. In one study of an EAP in a large corporation in Chicago, Maiden and Tolman (1989) used a case record review protocol to assess the presence of family violence in EAP cases. They found that 80% of cases in which substance abuse was involved also were likely to have some type of family violence involvement. In a substantial percentage of cases, family violence was identified but not dealt with directly in the EAP setting.

A few reports have been published in the press about workplace interventions in domestic violence (see, for example, Fredo, 1984; Freudenheim, 1988). At least one firm, Responses Inc. of Minneapolis, was specifically established to work closely with internal company EAPs and human resource departments. Responses helped employers deal with domestic violence cases among their employees by working to coordinate the provision of public and private services to families in which abuse was occurring.

It would seem that much more could be provided through coordinated efforts between social service agencies, EAPs, and employers. Preventive education of employees through posters, brochures, internal newsletter stories, and other educational materials could provide a large number of people with information to which they may not otherwise have access. Another educational effort might be for an employer to provide publicity and employee release time to attend educational lectures or workshops offered by social service agencies in the place of employment.

Most employers are probably not willing to provide comprehensive, on-site social services but there are steps beyond simple dissemination of information and workshops that might be developed. Many employers may already informally assist employees to connect with services or find temporary shelter. Responses Inc. has shown that such efforts may be formalized. EAPs might also be expanded beyond a sometimes narrow focus on chemical abuse problems. Including assessment and referral in woman abuse cases in the work of EAPs might not only enhance the ability of employees to make connections with needed services but also enhance worker productivity. In some cases, employers might also offer emergency grants or loans as a way of assisting employees in finding shelter or treatment. There are infinite possibilities in the workplace, and this setting is possibly the least explored to date.

These isolated efforts in the workplace, school systems, religious groups, and hospitals are evidence of the potential for change in these social systems. Much more is possible and perhaps the best current example of the changes possible can be found in criminal justice systems.

❑ Criminal Justice Interventions

Historically, the criminal justice system, including both police and courts, has been viewed as the major social institution charged with enforcing social values as expressed in law. Unfortunately, this system, as indicated in a number of studies, has seldom enforced assault statutes against a man on behalf of his intimate partner. For example, Ford (1983) found that prosecution of woman abusers was "governed as much by chance as by rational procedures" (p. 463). In his study of 325 battered women who *sought* prosecution, he found that only 30 of their cases eventually reached the court for a hearing. Similarly, Dutton (1987) estimated that, in the studies he reviewed, perpetrators of woman abuse had only "a 0.38% chance of being punished by the courts" (p. 189).

A disinterested criminal justice system has given both men who batter and their victims a clear message: No one will interfere with your domestic disputes. From a social learning perspective, this message is a reinforcing consequence. The absence of sanctions imposed by social institutions combined with the immediate rewards that violence often achieves make it likely that the batterer will maintain or even increase his use of violence in the future. Such inaction on the part of the criminal justice system sets the stage for a situation in which the violent man will feel no social restraint concerning his use of violence against women partners.

This situation has led many battered women's activists to view the criminal justice system as a major focus of their efforts. Implementation of quick and consistent sanctions against woman abuse by all components of the criminal justice system is seen as a necessary ingredient in successful efforts to end it (Pence, 1983). In ecological terms, this entails working at the level of a man's exosystem to bring about congruent social responses by many parts of his mesosystem.

To achieve this goal, advocates for battered women have developed a new type of organization, the Community Intervention Project (CIP). This section provides an overview of model CIP efforts, a discussion of policy and practice issues regarding coordinated efforts, and a brief review of current evidence concerning the effectiveness of CIPs.

COMMUNITY INTERVENTION PROJECTS

CIPs aim to coordinate various components of the criminal justice system in an effort to deliver to violent men clear and consistent sanctions in cases of woman abuse. Several dozen CIPs have been established in the United States (see Denver Domestic Violence Manual Task Force, 1988; Goolkasian, 1986; Soler, 1987; Soler & Martin, 1983) and exist in a variety of forms ranging from independent nonprofit organizations to programs of existing victim services within city or county attorneys' offices. Most CIPs are independent, nonprofit organizations staffed by legal advocates. Advocates assist individual battered women in their interactions with the criminal justice system and work at a systems level to change policies and procedures regarding all battered women.

Several of the country's first CIPs are located in Minnesota. The best known are the Domestic Abuse Intervention Project (DAIP) in Duluth (Pence, 1983; Pence & Shepard, 1988) and the several CIPs administered by the Domestic Abuse Project (DAP) in the Minneapolis metropolitan area (Brygger & Edleson, 1987; Gamache, Edleson, & Schock, 1988). Both DAIP and DAP operate as independent, nonprofit organizations and have been widely emulated in other jurisdictions. These "Minnesota models" will be the primary basis of the remainder of this chapter but other efforts will be highlighted as well.

Ecological context in which CIPs developed. Understanding the ecological context in which CIPs have developed provides important insights into their current design. A review of the literature on intervention with men who batter (Eisikovits & Edleson, 1989) indicated that, during the past two decades, a great deal of attention was given to changing police department responses to a variety of community events, including domestic violence. Evolving police responses to woman battering have been grouped into two categories: counseling oriented and arrest oriented (Homant, 1985). Through the 1970s and into the early 1980s, the actions of police in response to domestic disputes were primarily "family crisis intervention" oriented. Officers began to receive training in family mediation, and specialized crisis intervention units were created that paired social workers with a responding officer. This changing and expanded role of police was, at the time, consistent with the public's desire for more responsive police departments.

The early 1980s brought new pressures to bear on police departments. Pressures from victim rights groups and women's organizations grew and their agendas converged to bring about a major shift in criminal justice system responses to woman abuse. Victim rights advocates pushed for more severe punishment of offenders by courts and involvement of the victims in the process. Police who arrested perpetrators of violence on the street but did not arrest them for similar violence in the home were seen by women's groups as perpetuating both domestic violence and the unequal treatment of women. Added force was applied through successful suits against police inaction brought by several battered women around the country (e.g., *Thurman v. City of Torrington*, 1984).

The foci of research studies shifted as these new pressures began to intensify. Studies of actual and perceived deterrence showed that, of several possible forms of deterrence, police arrest was most effective in lowering recidivism (Sherman & Berk, 1984) and was perceived by violent men as the most severe sanction but one very unlikely to be employed (Carmody & Williams, 1987).

Increased public pressures, landmark cases, and renewed research support for deterrence theory have led to a dramatically increased use of arrest by police. As a result, ever increasing numbers of offenders are being sent to the court system for arraignment, trial, and sentencing.

For the first time, prosecutors and judges are now being forced to deal directly with large numbers of domestic violence cases. In the court system, the interests of victim rights advocates and women's groups have again converged. The push for attention to victim rights has reinforced pressure from women's groups to increase the use of battered women's wishes when making court decisions. In courts, however, the implementation of deterrent punishment such as a jail sentence is often avoided through stayed sentences or pretrial diversion. Instead, most courts favor taking a rehabilitation approach by diverting or mandating batterers into treatment.

> *Most courts favor a rehabilitation approach by diverting or mandating batterers into treatment.*

In summary, public attitudes appear to have changed; several land-mark cases have created new guidelines for police responses to men who batter; combined pressure from victim and battered women's advocates has increased; and research on both police actions during domestic calls and on victims' roles in the court process appears to have led to a greater readiness on the part of police, prosecutors, judges, and probation officers to respond to efforts such as CIPs. In many localities, this has brought about a sometimes dramatic shift in batterers' interactions with criminal justice professionals.

It is interesting that the use of deterrence by police and stayed sentencing by the court conditional upon completion of mandated rehabilitation is advocated by many CIPs (see Brygger & Edleson, 1987; Pence, 1983). While seemingly inconsistent, this approach ap-pears to offer perpetrators clear and immediate sanctions through arrest, conviction, sentencing (deterrence), and, later, motivation to enter treatment to avoid serving a jail sentence (rehabilitation).

Underlying beliefs in CIP design. These historical events influenced the basic design of most CIPs. In part, CIPs aim to revise macrosyste-mic beliefs as expressed by the criminal justice system. These re-vised beliefs are based on a feminist analysis and attempt to reframe popular thinking about both the causes of woman battering and the types of intervention goals desirable in response to such events (see Gamache et al., 1988).

Three particular beliefs, consistent with our viewpoint through-out this book, can be found underlying the design of many CIPs. First, it is assumed that all persons have a right to live free of vio-lence and, in the reverse, no one has the right to use violence except to remove him- or herself, in self-defense, from a physical assault. Second, woman abuse is believed to be rooted in the chronosystem and expressed in macrosystemic norms that permit males, as a class, to use violence to maintain their power and control over women and children. Finally, if woman battering is rooted in societal norms, then social systems must bear the responsibility for confronting men who batter and maximizing the protection of victims. Any attempt to effectively address the issue of woman battering must necessarily challenge these norms at all levels of the ecology.

These beliefs influence decisions about policy development, CIP procedures, and individual case management. Briefly, these design decisions generally include a focus on ending violence and seeking to have the societal systems involved confront perpetrators of violence, apply the same existing sanctions in dealing with woman abuse as they do in other assault cases, and remove the responsibility for confronting the assailant as much as possible from the victim who is often left to bear this burden alone. The success of these efforts are judged not only by their ability to maximize the protection available to victims but also their ability to empower battered women and minimize further danger or victimization.

The above guidelines have developed in the context of CIPs working to coordinate criminal justice with social service systems. They would appear, however, directly applicable in the analysis of other social system interventions and in the evaluation of each intervention's ability to respond consistently and effectively to battering.

Intervention project procedures. The way CIPs operate on a day-to-day basis is greatly influenced by the above belief systems and by a political climate focused on women's and victim's rights. One result has been widespread efforts to alter state legislation regarding woman abuse. For example, statewide coalitions for battered women have, since the 1970s, led to a series of successful lobbying efforts to change state laws regarding probable cause arrest, the levels at which woman battering crimes are charged, the terms under which restraining orders or orders for protection (OFPs) are issued, child support and custody considerations, and others. A number of statewide coalitions have also successfully lobbied for state funding of a variety of CIPs and other domestic violence programs. As a result, much of the underlying legal framework and core funding for such programs have been secured at a state level.

While a number of states—such as Minnesota—have depended heavily upon state-level changes in legislation, other communities have created similar coordinated efforts without such legislative changes. Some local communities have taken assault statutes already in place and worked for more consistent enforcement of them. In fact, legal advocates often gain the cooperation of criminal justice system components by arguing that they only seek the enforcement of assault statutes already on the books.

Most CIPs have set out to establish a network of new policies and procedures within criminal justice systems and social service agencies to which men are referred following prosecution. These efforts most often start with the local police department. In each CIP community, advocates work to obtain agreements with the local police administration to adopt policies requiring that officers make an arrest when probable cause exists that a domestic assault has occurred or when a restraining or protection order has been violated.

Once an arrest has been made, the police department will often agree to immediately notify the local CIP office. To offer the women increased protection, local jails also often agree to hold the men for several hours or until an arraignment is made the next morning. During this time, trained paid or volunteer advocates may be dispatched for separate visits to both the victim and, where permitted, the assailant. Male volunteers, some of whom are former batterers, visit the jail and attempt to provide encouragement for the man to acknowledge the severe negative results of his violent behavior, provide information about the range of treatment options available in the community, and offer support in seeking help through the court process. A pair of volunteer women's advocates attempt, at the same time, to offer help to the victim by visiting her at home while the man is in jail. During such visits or over the telephone, advocates provide support and information about subsequent court proceedings, shelters, and other services available to her. Time permitting, advocates also attempt to contact and provide services to women in homes where police have intervened but where an arrest did not occur.

CIP advocates frequently work with prosecuting attorneys in each community in an effort to establish procedures for handling battering cases and to work out agreements whereby prosecutors will aggressively pursue these cases when an arrest occurs or a complaint is filed. With the victim's permission, CIP advocates will assist prosecutors by supplying victim information during the court process. The goal at this point is to obtain judicial outcomes that will facilitate ending the violence and increase both the victim's safety and her satisfaction with the criminal justice system's response.

Upon entry of a guilty plea by the man or his conviction by the court, judges participate in the coordinated efforts by agreeing to order presentence investigations. During these investigations, probation officers participate by agreeing to incorporate information regarding the history of the man's violence and the battered woman's wishes into their presentence recommendations to the court. Where intervention projects exist, judges and referees are often asked to pronounce a sentence that includes imprisonment and then to stay part or all of the sentence pending successful completion of a batterers' treatment program as a condition of probation.

Throughout these legal proceedings, advocates attempt to work closely with and on behalf of the battered woman. They work with prosecutors and probation officers and assist victims to secure or renew orders for protection, temporary custody, and child support. They also try to help the women link up with shelter, community-based support and education groups, postshelter housing, job training programs, and the like.

Typically, the criminal justice system in communities where CIPs exist mandates men to receive specialized batterers' treatment. These specialized programs participate in CIPs by giving priority to men referred by court order and by submitting regular reports on each man's progress in counseling. Where men's treatment programs are inadequate or unavailable, CIP advocates work with local mental health agencies and professionals to developed a violence-focused program. Ideally, advocates continue to monitor each man's compliance with probation conditions and regularly report to the court on his progress in treatment.

The network of relationships within the criminal justice and social service systems is complex. Figure 6.1 illustrates, albeit in simplified and ideal terms, the processes described above.

STRATEGIES FOR DEVELOPING CIPS

The complex set of policies and procedures outlined above do not develop quickly. They are the result of months, if not years, of detailed work in a variety of settings. The experiences of existing programs offer several insights for those attempting to establish and maintain a program. A recent survey of 31 rural domestic violence

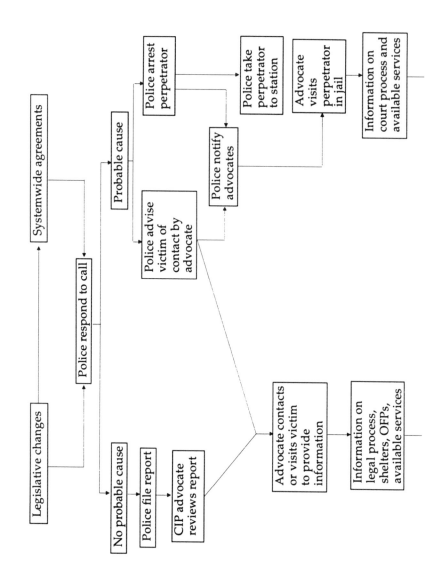

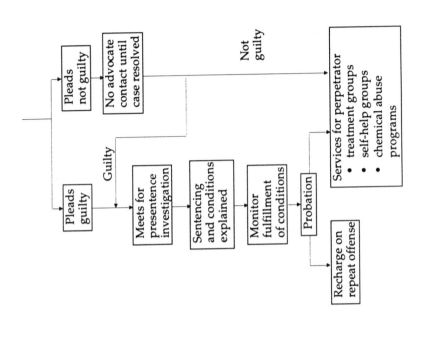

Pleads not guilty

No advocate contact until case resolved

Not guilty

Pleads guilty

Guilty

Meets for presentence investigation

Sentencing and conditions explained

Monitor fulfillment of conditions

Probation

Recharge on repeat offense

Services for perpetrator
- treatment groups
- self-help groups
- chemical abuse programs

With victim's permission, advocate readies data on abuse for relay to prosecutor

Continued advocate contact with victim concerning
- needs and services
- court process
- transportation and child care for court
- desired outcomes relayed to prosecutor

Services for battered women
- shelters
- postshelter housing
- job training
- self-help groups
- action groups
- legal assistance

Figure 6.1. Advocates' Roles in System Coordination

123

programs (Edleson & Frank, 1991) highlighted the following four development strategies that program staff repeatedly discussed: (a) Assess community needs carefully; (b) maintain high visibility in the community; (c) carefully develop cooperative relationships; and (d) expect change to occur slowly. While these programs included a variety of agencies, a number of these were CIPs and their strategies appear important to consider here.

Assess community needs. The 31-program survey (Edleson & Frank, 1991) found that staff repeatedly discussed the importance of understanding the culture of a particular community and of tailoring one's approach to the needs of the community. Respondents suggested that "talking to lots of people in your area, listening to what they have to say" is an important first step. In one area, teams of advocates and formerly battered women visited a variety of agencies to inform them about their project's work. In turn, the meetings yielded a great deal of information about possible future linkages between agencies.

In another example, after talking with many professionals, one program found that violence was often accepted or covered up by the very professionals with whom they were working to build intervention networks. This program's initial strategy then aimed to change the attitudes of professionals in its area. Another program became cautious about establishing a court-watch project to monitor judges' decisions after assessing that such activities might result in negative outcomes due to the judges' attitudes about outside monitoring.

Maintain high visibility. Program staff also frequently mentioned the need to be highly visible. Suggestions included the following: "Use all media, [put] signs in bathrooms [and] at offices of human service providers." "When starting a program it is important to get information out on the program. Send cards and brochures to clergy, doctors' offices, police departments, and attorneys."

Many programs maintained high visibility by having their own staff serve on the board of directors of other organizations such as community mental health centers and crime-victim centers. For similar reasons, some programs purposefully chose a cross section of the local community to serve on their own boards.

Develop cooperative relationships. Gaining the cooperation of police officers, prosecutors, judges, probation officers, and social service professionals is a time-consuming and resource-intensive process. Changing attitudes requires CIPs to engage in continual advocacy and monitoring during which consistent and clear community sanctions for violent behavior are repeatedly negotiated. This is especially true in large metropolitan areas where regular monitoring of hundreds of criminal justice professionals involved in many levels of handling domestic violence cases may be required.

This complexity may result in sporadic adherence by criminal justice systems to agreed upon policies. For example, Ferraro (1989) found that police in one Arizona community made arrests in only 18% of woman abuse cases despite the fact that there was a presumptive arrest policy in place. Similarly, Balos and Trotzky (1988) found that, despite a state requirement that men violating domestic restraining orders be arrested, very few violators were ever arrested.

To resolve these problems, CIP staff report a continual process of letting community leaders know who they are, what they are doing, and what the leaders can do to help control violence. Many CIPs have carefully identified and contacted key people in the community who might be instrumental in making policy or procedural changes. Programs in smaller communities report that access to such key people is often based on personal friendships. In some communities, church-based women's groups have also been particularly helpful to CIP staff in gaining access to community decision makers. This is the hard work of building a supportive network of individuals both within and outside systems who are willing and able to influence their future directions.

Many times, an individual police officer or county attorney will take an interest in the issue of woman abuse and make it his or her personal project to advance desired changes within the criminal justice system. In the early stages of development, this can be very helpful. In the longer term, however, the goal of CIP staff will be to build a larger network of support within the system and to have changes incorporated into daily operations and institutional policies.

Expect change to be slow. Many programs in our survey referred to the significant amount of time needed for change to take place. One advocate stated: "It takes time to develop a program and to gain community acceptance, trust, and respect."

Even when significant change does occur, it can have unintended results that may potentially set back gains already made. For example, the shortage of space in local jails and the backlog of cases awaiting prosecution create difficult issues with which CIPs are forced to deal. Recently, in an effort to lessen crowding in local jails, several officials of a local criminal justice system proposed changes to ease jail crowding, such as shorter jail stays following arrest, that advocates viewed as increasing the risks battered women already faced. After having spent years advocating for increased arrests, CIP staff had to organize against counterpressures to revert to earlier responses that did not require substantial jail space. This is just one example of how advocates are repeatedly forced to expend resources on simply maintaining changes already in place.

In another example of change that comes slowly, some CIPs have argued with prosecutors over what constitutes consistent but empowering social responses. As stated earlier, empowerment of women in society and particularly of battered women is a strong value common among many CIPs. Thus CIP efforts aim not only to maximize the protection available to victims and but also to empower battered women and minimize further danger or victimization. At the same time, prosecutors seek winnable cases, what Rauma (1984) calls "going for the gold." In their efforts to win a case, a number of prosecutors have suggested (see Lerman, 1986) that battered women unwilling to testify against their perpetrators be served a subpoena to force them to do so. Such recommendations are sometimes intended to relieve the woman of the responsibility (and blame) for deciding to testify. Forcing a battered woman to testify is seen by many advocates as disempowering and revictimizing women who are already in low power positions. A study by Ford (1984) supports these advocates' view. Ford found that battered women viewed control over the court process as a power resource used in negotiating a resolution with their partners. Removing the woman's control over the process through subpoenas and forcing her to testify may, in fact, lessen the usefulness of court to battered women.

Recently, some localities have begun to subpoena battered women after their second failure to voluntarily appear in court to testify. Some localities have also adopted a policy of dismissing a case if the woman fails to show after being subpoenaed, regardless of the circumstances. To win their cases, some defense attorneys have been found advising abusers to keep their partners away from the court in order to invoke the dismissal rule. In another extreme case, one judge ordered the police to *actively* seek out and arrest several women who did not appear after being subpoenaed. Several battered women spent the weekend in jail after being arrested late on a Friday afternoon. These events are a sad example of how a policy intended to relieve battered women of the decision to testify can easily be turned against them.

Sadly, another factor that slows change is biased or discriminatory responses against both victims and perpetrators because of their race, sex, ethnic origin, sexual preference, or age. These responses are problems repeatedly confronted by advocates. As part of their monitoring and system change efforts, many advocates attempt to lessen the effects of discrimination at every step of social system responses. This is seen as particularly important when procedures are being implemented differentially based on a man's or woman's status. For example, given the number of calls to police, a greater number of arrests might occur in minority neighborhoods than in white ones or prosecutions may be lower among white perpetrators than black ones. Persistent monitoring of police, prosecutor, court, and probation activities and regular meetings with individual professionals and their supervisors thus become a major part of the slow process of change in which advocates engage.

Expect the unexpected. We have added a fifth strategy based on our own experiences. As programs grow, certain situations may develop that were completely unforseen at the start. For example, the success of CIPS has led to an ever growing number of men being arrested for woman battering offenses. Denver's CIP, Project Safeguard, reported receiving almost 400 new cases per month in 1988. In the

Minneapolis area, the rise in the number of arrest cases has also been staggering. In the first 16 months of operating CIPs in three suburban communities, the Domestic Abuse Project's three advocates received a total of 98 arrest cases (Gamache et al., 1988). Now, in the city of Minneapolis alone, there are more than 3,000 woman abuser arrests per year referred to the six advocates and one volunteer coordinator in the Minneapolis Intervention Project (MIP). These staggering numbers are being replicated across the country and overwhelming small CIP staffs. As a result, CIP advocates have been forced to prioritize individual cases and the system changes on which they work. They have, however, resisted calls for greater use of diversion prior to conviction in the fear that it allows the perpetrator to avoid the clear sanctions of conviction and a criminal record.

In an effort to assist a larger number of women with limited resources, the Domestic Abuse Project in Minneapolis experimented with a monitoring project in several suburban communities where CIPs did not yet exist. Paid and volunteer advocates accompanied police on domestic calls and monitored court proceedings on a regular basis. Monthly statistics were gathered on the total number of arrest cases, the percentage found guilty, and the percentage of cases dismissed. These data were then reported to all of the participating communities, providing police, prosecutors, and judges with detailed information on their system's response *in comparison* with that of the other communities. While the effects of this effort are still unclear, the hoped for outcome was that monitoring alone might create a substantial change in the systems observed and prove to be a less expensive option for some communities.

EMPIRICAL SUPPORT FOR CRIMINAL JUSTICE INTERVENTION

To date, very few evaluations of coordinated community interventions have been completed. Those that do exist can be grouped into three categories, including evaluations of (a) system-level activity change, (b) court-mandated batterers' treatment programs, and (c) coordination efforts.

System-level activity. While the number of arrested and prosecuted perpetrators appears to be rising dramatically around the country, only one study has linked coordination efforts to these system-level changes in activity. Gamache et al. (1988) retrospectively studied the first three communities in which the Domestic Abuse Project established CIPs. These communities were small, suburban cities in the Minneapolis metropolitan area (15,000 to 36,000 people) that were relatively homogeneous (97% white) and prosperous (70% to 80% held white collar positions). Archival police and court records were examined and charts constructed depicting changes in arrests, convictions, and perpetrators mandated to treatment by the courts. The data showed, both in visual and in statistical analyses, that CIPs had a significant impact on increasing arrests, convictions, and court mandates to treatment. These data also showed that the larger the system, the more difficult the coordination.

What these data did not indicate was the degree to which all of this significantly increased activity led to decreases in perpetration of violence against women. Other studies on court-mandated treatment and coordinated interventions do shed some light on this issue.

Court-mandated treatment. A number of studies have examined the effectiveness of court mandates and court-mandated batterers' treatment on recidivism of participating men (see Dutton, 1986; Parker & Saunders, 1989; Saunders & Parker, 1989; Shepard, 1987; Tolman & Bhosley, 1991). A number of these studies were reviewed in Chapter 4. Taken together, they indicate that court-mandated or recommended treatment may be an effective method of referring men to treatment and, if they complete the mandated treatment program, there is a likelihood that these men, as often as others, will end their use of violence during follow-up periods.

Coordinated efforts. The above studies allow only indirect inferences concerning the impact of coordinated community responses. System activity can be changed, and court involvement in referring men to counseling seems a mostly effective strategy. But, because such programs are relatively new, few studies are available that take into account the various operational factors described earlier.

Measuring the overall effect of Duluth's coordinated intervention in woman battering in Minnesota, Pence, Novack, and Galaway (1982) reported that, at 6 months after men completed a treatment program, 51% of victims reported no subsequent violence compared with 41% of a comparison group of victims from the same community. Unfortunately, the contributions of the various criminal justice and social service components were not tested.

Steinman (1988) has evaluated a coordinated community intervention effort in Nebraska and found that postarrest sanctions had little influence on recidivism beyond what was achieved through the initial arrest. There were some indications in these data that certain postarrest sanctions, such as fines, might be associated with lower rates of recidivism. To investigate these possible associations, Steinman (1990) conducted a second study that compared those cases that occurred prior to the implementation of the coordinated community effort and those that occurred after it was established. He found that police actions *not* coordinated with other sanctions produced increased violence. Police action, especially arrest, *in coordination* with other criminal justice efforts became a significant deterrent. Steinman also found, however, that coordinated efforts were not consistently effective and that victims who called the police themselves and who were not living with their perpetrator tended to be at increased risk of abuse. Bringing advocates, police, and others into the situation may put some women at a heightened level of risk. It may be, however, that these women already live in a high risk situation and that the violence being committed against them would be increasing regardless of criminal justice efforts.

Similar findings were reported in a recent study of 425 women who had been contacted by the Minneapolis police concerning a woman abuse report. Syers and Edleson (1991) found that police visits to the home, combined with an eventual arrest of the perpetrator that is *also* followed by court-mandated treatment, are significantly more likely than other combinations of criminal justice actions to end repeat incidents of violence.

These studies seem to indicate that *coordinated* criminal justice responses that include arrest policies and postarrest sanctions or treatment can be effective but that some women may face increased risks in actively seeking the aid of criminal justice professionals.

Ecologically, these studies offer empirical support for efforts aimed at enhancing the consistency of direct microsystem interactions with a man. They also support the idea that exosystem efforts to co-ordinate various criminal justice responses may create a mesosystem that is more powerful in influencing a man to end his violence than would be uncoordinated actions by the individual microsystems.

ISSUES IN COMMUNITY INTERVENTION

There are several issues that are often raised as criticisms of CIP projects. One is the apparent contradiction between a feminist analysis of the problem on one hand and, on the other hand, the use of predominantly male, power-based institutions such as the police to implement CIP goals. Thus battered women's advocates find themselves criticizing social institutions for the power imbalance between genders but then promoting programs that use this very power to intervene in woman abuse.

CIPs do focus on the use of criminal justice institutions. These same institutions have often been viewed as wielding power abusively, especially in the case of women and minorities (G. Sullivan, 1982). Battered women's advocates argue, however, that they are working to bring about a change in the way such power is used by the criminal justice system. The goal of CIPs is to see the system act consistently in a manner that does not discriminate against women, regardless of their relationship status. As pointed out earlier, many CIPs will monitor not only for bias against women in criminal justice responses but also for bias against minorities. Most CIPs see their roles as independent monitors and advocates of change as extremely important.

Until recently, a reliance on police use of arrest has been widely accepted by many as the most effective police action in domestic disturbance cases. This conclusion was partially based on the results of Sherman and Berk's (1984) widely publicized experiment that found arrest almost twice as effective as others actions in reducing recidivism among violent men. The results of a series of more recent studies that have attempted to replicate Sherman and Berk's findings have shed some doubt on those original findings. Funded by the National Institute of Justice, these studies sought to correct some of the weaknesses of Sherman and Berk's original findings and shed light on a large variety of factors that may contribute to successful police intervention. In two studies (Dunford, Huizinga, & Elliot, 1990; Hirschel, Hutchison, & Dean, 1992), arrest was found to be no more effective than other responses. In the third study (Sherman et al., 1991), neither those held a short time in custody nor those held longer following an arrest tended to be less likely to recidivate than those not arrested at all. These findings have accelerated the debates on overuse of force and on the use of crowded jails following an arrest.

One note of caution: Sherman et al. (1991) point out that only 5% of the men in their study were charged by the courts and only 1% were convicted. The conviction rate in at least one other study was also low. These studies do not therefore take into account the *combined* effects of coordinated community efforts as discussed in this section. Our research (Syers & Edleson, 1991) and that of Steinman (1990) has tended to show that *combined* criminal justice efforts do offer most women greater protection than when no arrest occurs.

The establishment of CIPs, with their heavy reliance on police, has also often been met with ambivalence in minority communities. Police have been and continue to be seen as especially abusive to minorities in general and to minority men in particular. A black woman who was battered by her husband tells the story of how she wanted the police to stop her husband's violence, but they instead came into her home and badly beat him after he had just beaten her. She felt she had only escalated the violence in her home by seeking help from the police. The Minneapolis Intervention Project, a CIP operated by the Domestic Abuse Project, has attempted to deal with these issues by supporting an ethnically diverse staff, by opening a satellite office in a neighborhood center that is frequently used by minority communities, by working especially hard to coordinate its activities with local, predominantly minority organizations, and by closely monitoring criminal justice system behavior for use of abusive tactics.

Another issue concerns the overuse of jails. Jails are often unhealthy environments and in many localities there is very limited space for holding criminals. Recognizing this, CIP staff often seek to have the man convicted of his crime and sentenced to jail time that is then stayed as long as he enrolls in and completes a group treatment program. CIPs, however, often resist efforts to divert violent men into treatment prior to trial and conviction. Violence is criminal behavior and it is considered important to create an ongoing record of a man's continuing offenses so that more severe sanctions may be imposed if subsequent incidents occur. In many localities, records will not be maintained if a man is diverted to treatment before trial.

As mandated treatment becomes a desired part of the process, the quality and content of such treatment programs also become an important issue. As many states and localities move to mandate larger numbers of men into batterers' treatment programs, a wide array of human service professionals and organizations are seeking to capitalize on this new source of clients. To ensure the quality of court-mandated treatment programs, some states and localities have adopted quality guidelines and lists of approved programs that meet certain standards (see County of Los Angeles, 1988; Denver Committee to Establish Treatment Standards, 1985).

Finally, there is a danger that CIPs will be co-opted by the criminal justice system (Sullivan, 1982). Increasingly, CIP budgets are being supplemented by tax dollars while other programs are being incorporated into city or county attorneys' offices. As this occurs, there is a distinct danger that CIPs will loose their independence and their ability both to monitor systems and to apply pressure for change. Already, some criticize the common practice of collecting witness data for prosecutors as doing the work that others should perform. It is not hard to envision programs that would be restricted to focusing solely on individual case advocacy, thereby becoming extensions of existing bureaucracies. It is important for CIPs to place continued emphasis on system change rather than becoming a permanent supplement to existing case management services.

❏ Summary

Social systems are a major focus of intervention with men who batter. Insufficient attention and funding have been offered innovative programs that seek to prevent violence through early intervention in educational, medical, employment, and religious systems. A few model programs have been reported, but much more is both possible and necessary.

To the contrary, intervention in the criminal justice system has received a great deal of attention. Despite some problems and criticisms, the number of CIPs is growing rapidly. The data we currently have about the effectiveness of such programs, while minimal, is encouraging. It does appear that coordinated efforts that include a variety of criminal justice actions may decrease the likelihood of repeat violence. The experience of CIPs indicates the importance of building networks not only within specific criminal justice systems but also across states and with legislative bodies.

Epilogue:
Toward a Violence-Free Ecology

We began this book with a discussion of our proposed integrated framework. Throughout the preceding chapters, we have attempted to discuss various forms of intervention within the context of this framework. We have examined individual, couple, group, and system change efforts. Each offers unique benefits and each presents a varying degree of potential problems.

Comparing our framework with existing U.S. interventions with men who batter points to the scarcity of larger system interventions in this country. It is striking that so many promote a macrosystem analysis in which social-structural issues are primary while so few have developed interventions focused on larger system change. For almost two decades, advocates for battered women have argued for system changes while the larger society has funneled an increasing proportion of resources and attention toward individual and family-based solutions (Davis, 1987). It is also striking that, when system change has occurred, it has been primarily focused on the criminal justice system. Few attempts have been made to coordinate existing responses within, for example, the employment, educational, health, religious, and mass media systems.

Perhaps this country's emphasis on microsystem intervention is a result of U.S. culture. As Dobash and Dobash (in press) argue: "In the United States, like no other country, extreme individualism coupled with a perpetual concern about one's status and position concomitant with unrestrained ideals of striving and success, are powerful forces in efforts to seek solutions through individual, in contrast to community, approaches" (p. 6).

The focus on individuals and those in the near environment has most often resulted in therapeutic interventions. Since the 1930s, the application of therapeutic approaches to social problems has mushroomed to the point where some have labeled the United States the "therapeutic society" (Dobash & Dobash, in press). The dramatically increasing number of psychological professionals is viewed as fueling a growth industry that focuses primarily on identifying and treating individuals rather than changing the social systems that create and maintain violence. This trend is clearly evident in the recent history of domestic violence as a social problem. Davis (1987) has documented how, during the past two decades, the definition of woman abuse has been transformed from a social problem created by society's historical treatment of women to one of individual relationship problems.

Another striking aspect of current interventions and the literature about them is their provincial nature. Seldom are references made to data about domestic violence or interventions in other cultures except for an occasional reference to Great Britain (see, for example, Dobash & Dobash, 1987). Yet, the United Nations is working with countries around the world to enhance women's rights and end their oppression based on violence (United Nations, 1987). Data are available on domestic violence in a number of countries worldwide including India (Singh, 1986), Bangladesh (Akanda & Shamim, 1985), Papua New Guinea (McDowell, 1990; Mitchell, 1990; Scaglion, 1990), New Zealand (Fergusson, Horwood, Kershaw, & Shannon, 1986), Japan (Kumagai, 1979, 1981), and Finland and Sweden (Peltoniemi, 1982). Worldwide interventions to end violence against women are regularly reported in publications such as *Link*, published by the Commonwealth Secretariat in London; *The Women's Watch*, published by the International Women's Rights Action Watch in Minneapolis, Minnesota; and *WIN News*, published by the Women's International Network in Lexington, Massachusetts. These interventions include the establishment of special police offices in Brazil that deal only with issues of violence against women (see Riding, 1985), a videotape using traditional puppetry to communicate about domestic violence that has been produced by the Indian government, a network of women from eight Southeast Asian countries who have developed publications for battered women and their advocates (see Women's Crisis Centre, 1990), and grass-roots efforts in a number of countries including Israel (Edleson, Eisikovits, & Peled, 1991) and Germany (Kappel & Leuteritz, 1980).

Viewing the current network of interventions through an ecological lens and expanding our vision to include the experiences of those in other cultures may lead us toward a variety of intervention efforts that have yet to be established on a wide scale. For example, one might consider a national effort to present the issues of woman abuse through folk art and theater such as was done in India with the development of a videotape using traditional puppets. Another approach might be to develop a neighborhood monitoring system modeled after Chinese block councils and U.S. crime prevention programs. It is also possible to envision community intervention projects (CIPs) being expanded beyond the criminal justice system to intervene in employment, medical, educational, religious, and mass media systems.

Syers-McNairy's (1990) recent study points out that battered women seeking to build lives free of their violent partners draw upon multiple systems. Acknowledging that battered women must negotiate multiple systems, Sullivan (1991) has recently reported pilot data on an intervention project in which advocates helped women leaving abusive partners. Unique to this study was the fact that advocacy was provided across multiple systems, not just within the criminal justice system. Women exiting battered women's shelters were assisted for 10 weeks by trained paraprofessional advocates in obtaining resources from financial, health care, educational, and other systems. Such advocacy might enhance the effectiveness of currently available services through coordinating efforts of different systems and providing guidance to those seeking to access them.

One might envision CIPs following Sullivan's model, where intervention to stop abuse would occur across multiple systems. Another variant could be to expand specialized intervention projects into other systems. For example, a CIP might be established that works on a regular basis with entire school systems. The response of the entire system would be coordinated with the aim of ending violence and models of violence. Distinct intervention and advocacy would be brought to bear in specific cases of violence. Curricula might be revised or developed and integrated into lesson plans. Special training of teachers and supporting professionals could take place. Course electives concerning relationships and violence could also be offered. Media and outreach campaigns that regularly communicate about violence and the abuse of power might also be developed within the school environment.

To create violence-free ecologies we must promote multiple system interventions.

If our goal is to create violence-free ecologies, we must promote multiple-system interventions. One need only look at the success in some localities of efforts to reduce deaths due to automobile accidents. Some states, such as Minnesota, have witnessed mortality rates due to such accidents cut almost in half in less than a decade. Such successes are probably the result of a combination of factors including changes in automobile and road designs, reduced speed limits that are strictly enforced, major efforts by groups such as Mothers Against Drunk Driving (MADD) to change social attitudes and behavior patterns concerning drinking and driving, large-scale media exposure to the issue, programs offering free taxi and bus service on holidays such as New Year's Eve, new laws establishing the responsibility of businesses to curtail the extreme drinking behavior of customers, and severe punishment for those who violate laws prohibiting drunk driving.

It could be argued, however, that multisystem efforts actually work within a series of individual systems and are not much different than working with individual perpetrators of violence or their families. In the end, it is not the violence that is the central issue. It is the abuse of power by men through violence against women that is established and maintained as an acceptable practice within our society. Is it not the current economic, political, and patriarchal structures, or macrosystem blueprints as Bronfenbrenner (1979) might call them, that continue to maintain such abuses of power?

We agree with this argument to a certain extent. Unless change occurs in the underlying blueprints that guide the social development of individuals and larger social units, it is hard to envision how a violence-free ecology is possible. On the other hand, rejecting efforts short of restructuring the entire macrosystem as too narrowly focused seems unwise. It is not clear to us that change can only occur from the top down. It seems entirely possible that change can be brought about in a variety of ways. Ecological efforts to change the

> *Efforts to change the systems in which people are socialized may subsequently lead to macrosystem change.*

systems in which people are socialized and live on a daily basis may subsequently, in fact, lead to macrosystem change.

We discussed earlier, in Chapter 1, how popular societal beliefs about a particular problem tend to evolve over time and expand the range of possible interventions a society may consider feasible. Reversing this notion, it seems possible that changes in the way social systems respond could, in turn, lead to revised macrosystem blueprints for a society. This may be part of the reason for dramatic decreases in the number of accident deaths involving intoxicated drivers in some localities.

We began the book with a quote from Gandhi, who asserts that the road to nonviolence must begin at home and must begin as an individual effort. Gandhi also wrote, however, that poverty is the worst form of violence. These two statements by Gandhi illustrate that work on a violence-free ecology must focus on all levels of the ecology, from individual changes in behavior to changes in economic arrangements that end poverty and inequality worldwide. Our hope is that the integrated framework we have presented and the multiple forms of intervention we have described may help others to envision, design, and implement new forms of intervention in their communities. It is also our hope that this, in turn, may help accelerate the evolution of social thought and attitudes concerning the distribution of power and how it is both used and abused in our society.

References

Adams, D. C. (1988). Treatment models of men who batter: A pro-feminist analysis. In K. Yllo & M. Bograd (Eds.), *Feminist perspectives on wife abuse* (pp. 176-199). Newbury Park, CA: Sage.

Adams, D. C. (1989). Feminist-based interventions for battering men. In L. Caesar & L. K. Hamberger (Eds.), *Treating men who batter: Theory, practice and programs* (pp. 3-23). New York: Springer.

Adams, D. C., & McCormick, A. J. (1982). Men unlearning violence: A group approach based on the collective model. In M. Roy (Ed.), *The abusive partner* (pp. 170-197). New York: Van Nostrand Reinhold.

Akanda, L., & Shamin, I. (1985). *Women and violence: A comparative study of rural and urban violence against women in Bangladesh.* Dhaka, Bangladesh: Women for Women: A Research & Study Group.

Alsdurf, J. M. (1985). Wife abuse and the church: The response of pastors. *Response, 8,* 9-11.

Balos, B. & Trotzky, K. (1988). Enforcement of the Domestic Abuse Act in Minnesota: A preliminary study. *Law & Inequality, 6,* 83-125.

Bandura, A. (1973). *Aggression: A social learning analysis.* Englewood Cliffs, NJ: Prentice-Hall.

Bandura, A. (1977). *Social learning theory.* Englewood Cliffs, NJ: Prentice-Hall.

Bankovics, G., & Kittel, J. (1983). *Couple's treatment outline.* Unpublished manuscripts, Domestic Abuse Project, Minneapolis, MN.

Barling, J., & Rosenbaum, A. (1986). Work stressors and wife abuse. *Journal of Applied Psychology, 71*(2), 346-348.

Barnett, O. W., & Planeaux, P. S. (1989, January). *A hostility-guilt assessment of counseled and uncounseled batterers.* Paper presented at the Responses to Family Violence Research Conference, Purdue University.

Bass, B. (1973). An unusual behavioral technique for treating obsessive ruminations. *Psychotherapy: Theory, Research, and Practice, 10,* 191-192.

Bauer, C., & Ritt, L. (1983). "A husband is a beating animal": Frances Power Cobbe confronts the wife-abuse problem in Victorian England. *International Journal of Women's Studies, 6,* 99-118.

Beck, A. T. (1976). *Cognitive therapy and the emotional disorders.* New York: International Universities Press.

Beck, A. T., Ward, C. H., Mendelson, M., Mock, J., & Erbaugh, J. (1961). An inventory for measuring depression. *Archives of General Psychiatry, 4,* 53-63.

Bograd, M. (1984). Family systems approaches to wife battering: A feminist critique. *American Journal of Orthopsychiatry, 54,* 558-568.

Bograd, M. (1986). Holding the line: Confronting the abusive partner. *The Family Therapy Networker, 10,* 44-47.

Bograd, M. (1988). Feminist perspectives on wife abuse. In K. Yllo & M. Bograd (Eds.), *Feminist perspectives on wife abuse* (pp. 11-26). Newbury Park, CA: Sage.

Bowker, L. H. (1982). *Beating wife-beating.* Lexington, MA: D. C. Heath.

Bronfenbrenner, U. (1977). Toward an experimental ecology of human development. *American Psychologist, 32,* 523-531.

Bronfenbrenner, U. (1979). *The ecology of human development: Experiments by nature and design.* Cambridge, MA: Harvard University Press.

Bronfenbrenner, U. (1986). Ecology of the family as a context for human development: Research perspectives. *Developmental Psychology, 22,* 723-742.

Brygger, M. P., & Edleson, J. L. (1987). The Domestic Abuse Project: A multisystems intervention in woman battering. *Journal of Interpersonal Violence, 2,* 324-336.

Bureau of Justice Statistics. (1980). *Intimate victims: A study of violence among friends and relatives* (Publication No. DD062319). Washington, DC: U.S. Department of Justice.

Buss, A. H., & Durkee, A. (1957). An inventory for assessing different kinds of hostility. *Journal of Clinical and Counsulting Psychology, 21,* 343-349.

Butcher, J., & Koss, M. (1978). Research on brief and crisis-oriented therapies. In S. Garfield & A. Bergin (Eds.), *Handbook of psychotherapy and behavior change* (2nd ed.). New York: John Wiley.

Caesar, P. L. (1985, August). *The wife-beater: Personality and psychosocial characteristics.* Paper presented at the meeting of the American Psychological Association, Los Angeles, CA.

Campbell, J. C., & Sheridan, D. J. (1989). Emergency nursing interventions with battered women. *Journal of Emergency Nursing, 15,* 12-17.

Carlson, B. E. (1984). Causes and maintenance of domestic violence: An ecological analysis. *Social Service Review, 58,* 569-587.

Carmody, D. C., & Williams, K. R. (1987). Wife assault and perceptions of sanctions. *Violence and Victims, 2,* 25-38.

Coleman, K. H. (1980). Conjugal violence: What 33 men report. *Journal of Marital and Family Therapy, 6,* 207-213.

Cook, D. R., & Frantz-Cook, A. (1984). A systemic treatment approach to wife battering. *Journal of Marital and Family Therapy, 10,* 83-93.

County of Los Angeles. (1988). *Batterer's treatment program guidelines.* Los Angeles, CA: County Department of Community and Senior Citizens Services.

Davidson, T. (1977). Wifebeating: A recurring phenomenon throughout history. In M. Roy (Ed.), *Battered women* (pp. 2-23). New York: Van Nostrand Reinhold.

Davis, L. V. (1987). Battered women: The transformation of a social problem. *Social Work, 32,* 306-311.

DeMaris, A., & Jackson, J. K. (1987). Batterers reports of recidivism after counseling. *Social Casework, 68*(8), 458-465.

Denver Committee to Establish Treatment Standards. (1985). *Standards for the treatment of domestic violence perpetrators.* Denver, CO: City of Denver.

Denver Domestic Violence Manual Task Force. (1988). *The Denver Domestic Violence Manual.* Denver, CO: City of Denver.

Deschner, J. P. (1984). *The hitting habit: Anger control for battering couples.* New York: Free Press.

Deschner, J., & McNeil, J. (1984). *Lowering the drop-out rate for groups for battering couples.* Paper presented at the Symposium for the Advancement of Social Work With Groups, Chicago, Illinois.

Deschner, J. P., & McNeil, J. S. (1986). Results of anger control training for battering couples. *Journal of Family Violence, 1*(2), 111-120.

Deschner, J. P., McNeil, J. S., & Moore, M. G. (1986). A treatment model for batterers. *Social Casework, 67,* 55-60.

Devore, W., & Schlesinger, E. G. (1987). *Ethnic-sensitive social work practice.* Columbus, OH: Charles E. Merrill.

Dobash, R. E., & Dobash, R. P. (1979). *Violence against wives.* New York: Free Press.

Dobash, R. E., & Dobash, R. P. (1987). The response of the British and American women's movements to violence against women. In J. Hanmer & M. Maynard (Eds.), *Women, violence, and social context* (pp. 169-179). Atlantic Highlands, NJ: Humanities Press International.

Dobash, R. E., & Dobash, R. P. (1992). *Women, violence and social change .* New York: Routledge.

Douglas, M. A., Alley, J., Daston, A. P., Svaldi-Farr, J., & Samson, M. (1984, August). *Court-involved batterers and their victims: Characteristics and ethnic differences.* Paper presented at the 92nd Annual Convention of the American Psychological Association, Toronto, Canada.

Douglas, M. A., & Perrin, S. (1987, July). *Recidivism and accuracy of self-reported violence and arrest.* Paper presented at the Third National Conference for Family Violence Researchers, University of New Hampshire, Durham.

Duncan-Jones, P., & Henderson, S. (1978). The use of a two-phase design in a population study. *Social Psychiatry, 13,* 231-237.

Dunford, F. W., Huizinga, D., & Elliot, D. S. (1990). The role of arrest in domestic assault: The Omaha Police Experiment. *Criminology, 28,* 183-206.

Dutton, D. G. (1985). An ecologically nested theory of male violence toward intimates. *International Journal of Women's Studies, 8,* 404-413.

Dutton, D. G. (1986). The outcome of court-mandated treatment for wife assault: A quasi-experimental evaluation. *Violence and Victims, 1,* 163-175.

Dutton, D. G. (1987). The criminal justice response to wife assault. *Law and Human Behavior, 11,* 189-206.

Dutton, D. G. (1988). *The domestic assault of women.* Boston, MA: Allyn & Bacon.

Dutton, D. G., & Browning, J. J. (1987). Power struggles and intimacy anxieties as causative factors of violence in intimate relationships. In G. Russell (Ed.) *Violence in intimate relationships.* New York: Sage.

Dutton, D. G., & Strachan, C. E. (1987, July 6-9). *The prediction of recidivism in a population of wife assaulters.* Paper presented at the Third National Conference on Family Violence, Durham, NH.

Eddy, M., & Myers, T. (1984). *Helping men who batter: A profile of programs in the U.S.* Austin: Texas Department of Human Resources.

Edleson, J. L. (1984a). Working with men who batter. *Social Work, 29,* 237-242.

Edleson, J. L. (1984b). Violence is the issue: A critique of Neidig's assumptions. *Victimology, 9,* 483-489.

Edleson, J. L. (1990). Judging success in intervention with men who batter. In D. J. Besharov (Ed.), *Family violence: Research and public policy issues* (pp. 130-145). Washington, DC: American Enterprise Institute.

Edleson, J. L. (1991a). Social workers and battered women: A study of case records from 1907 to 1945. *Social Service Review, 65,* 304-313.

Edleson, J. L. (1991b). Coordinated community responses to woman battering. In M. Steinman (Ed.), *Woman battering: Policy responses* (pp. 203-219). Cincinnati, OH: Anderson.

Edleson, J. L., & Brygger, M. P. (1986). Gender differences in reporting of battering incidences. *Family Relations, 35,* 377-382.

Edleson, J. L., Eisikovits, Z. C., & Peled, E. (1991). A model for analyzing societal responses to woman battering: Israel as a case in point. *International Social Work, 35,* 19-33.

Edleson, J. L., & Frank, M. D. (1991). Rural interventions in woman battering: One state's strategies. *Families in Society, 72,* 543-551.

Edleson, J. L., & Grusznski, R. J. (1989). Treating men who batter: Four years of outcome data from the Domestic Abuse Project. *Journal of Social Service Research, 12,* 3-22.

Edleson, J. L., Miller, D. M., Stone, G. W., & Chapman, D. G. (1985). Group treatment for men who batter. *Social Work Research and Abstracts, 21,* 18-21.

Edleson, J. L., & Syers, M. (1990). The relative effectiveness of group treatments for men who batter. *Social Work Research and Abstracts, 26,* 10-17.

Edleson, J. L., & Syers, M. (1991). The effects of group treatment for men who batter: An 18-month follow-up study. *Research on Social Work Practice, 1,* 227-243.

Edwards, S. M. (1985). A socio-legal evaluation of gender ideologies in domestic violence assault and spousal homicides. *Victimology, 10,* 1-4.

Eisikovits, Z. C., & Edleson, J. L. (1989). Intervening with men who batter: A critical review of the literature. *Social Service Review, 63,* 384-414.

Eisikovits, Z. C., Guttmann, E., Sela-Amit, M., & Edleson, J. L. (1991). *Relationship adjustment, conflict, and social support in woman battering.* Manuscript submitted for publication.

Elbow, M. (1982). Children of violent marriages: The forgotten victims. *Social Casework, 63,* 465-471.

Ellis, A. (1970). *The essence of rational psychotherapy: A comprehensive approach to treatment.* New York: Institute for Rational Living.

EMERGE. (1981). *Organizing and implementing services for men who batter.* Boston: Author.

Ewing, W. (1987). Domestic violence and community health care ethics: Reflections on systemic intervention. *Family and Community Health, 10*, 54-62.

Ewing, W., Lindsey, M., & Pomerantz, J. (1984). *AMEND Manual for Helpers*. Denver, CO: AMEND.

Fagan, J. (1989). Cessation of family violence: Deterrence and dissuasion. In L. Ohlin & M. Tonry (Eds.), *Family violence* (pp. 377-425). Chicago: University of Chicago Press.

Fagan, J., Steward, D. K., & Hansen, H. (1983). Violent men or violent husbands? Background factors and situational correlates. In D. Finkelhor (Ed.), *The dark side of families*. Beverly Hills, CA: Sage.

Fantuzzo, J. W., & Lindquist, C. U. (1989). The effects of observing conjugal violence on children: A review and analysis of research methodology. *Journal of Family Violence, 4*, 77-94.

Faulkner, K., Stoltenberg, C., Cogan, R., Nolder, M., Shooter, G., & Garvin, R. (1988, August). *Are individuals in physically abusive relationships pathological, non-pathological, or both?* Paper presented at the meeting of the American Psychological Association, Atlanta, GA.

Feazell, C. S., Mayers, R. S., & Deschner, J. (1984). Services for men who batter: Implications for programs and policies. *Family Relations, 33*, 217-223.

Federal Bureau of Investigation. (1979). *Crime in the United States*. Washington, DC: Author.

Federal Bureau of Investigation. (1986). *Crime in the United States*. Washington, DC: Author.

Fergusson, D. M., Horwood, L. J., Kershaw, K. L., & Shannon, F. T. (1986). Factors associated with reports of wife assault in New Zealand. *Journal of Marriage and the Family, 48*, 407-412.

Ferraro, K. (1989). Policing woman battering. *Social Problems, 36*, 61-74.

Finkelhor, D., & Yllo, K. (1982). Forced sex in marriage: A preliminary research report. *Crime and Delinquency, 28*, 459-478.

Ford, D. A. (1983). Wife battery and criminal justice: A study of victim decision-making. *Family Relations, 32*, 463-475.

Ford, D. A. (1984, August). *Prosecution as a victim power resource for managing conjugal violence*. Paper presented at the annual meeting of the Society for the Study of Social Problems, San Antonio, TX.

Fortune, M. M., & Hertze, J. (1987). A commentary on religious issues in family violence. In M. Pellauer, B. Chester, & J. Boyajian (Eds.), *Sexual assault and abuse: A handbook for clergy and religious professionals* (pp. 67-83). New York: Harper & Row.

Foy, D. W., Eisler, R. M., & Pinkston, S. (1975). Modeled assertion in a case of explosive rage. *Journal of Behavior Therapy and Experimental Psychiatry, 6*, 135-137.

Frankl, V. E. (1959). *Man's search for meaning*. Boston: Beacon.

Fredo, M. (1984, January 26). When violence at home affects work. *The New York Times*, p. F17.

Fruedenheim, M. (1988, August 23). Employers act to stop family violence. *The New York Times, 137*, 1, 40.

Gallaway, B. (1985). Victim participation in the penal-corrective process. *Victimology, 10*, 617-630.

Gamache, D. J., Edleson, J. L., & Schock, M. D. (1988). Coordinated police, judicial and social service response to woman battering: A multi-baseline evaluation across three communities. In G. T. Hotaling, D. Finkelhor, J. T. Kirkpatrick, & M. Straus (Eds.), *Coping with family violence: Research and policy perspectives* (pp. 193-209). Newbury Park, CA: Sage.

Gambrill, E. D. (1977). *Behavior modification: Handbook of assessment, intervention, and evaluation.* San Francisco: Jossey-Bass.

Gandhi, M. K. (1942). The best field for Ahimsa. In M. K. Gandhi (Ed.) *Non-violence in peace & war* (Vol. 1, pp. 299-300). Ahmedabad, India: Navajivan Publishing House.

Ganley, A. L. (1981). *Court mandated counseling for men who batter: A three-day workshop for mental health professionals.* Washington, DC: Center for Women Policy Studies.

Ganley, A. L. (1987). Perpetrators of domestic violence: An overview of counseling the court-mandated client. In D. J. Sonkin (Ed.), *Domestic violence on trial* (pp. 155-173). New York: Springer.

Ganley, A. L. (1989). Integrating feminist and social learning analyses of aggression: Creating multiple models for intervention with men who batter. In P. L. Caesar & L. K. Hamberger (Eds.), *Treatment of men who batter* (pp. 196-235). New York: Springer.

Ganley, A. L., & Harris, L. (1978, August). *Domestic violence: Issues in designing and implementing programs for male batterers.* Paper presented at the meeting of the American Psychological Association, Toronto, Ontario, Canada.

Garbarino, J., Guttmann, E., & Seeley, J. W. (1986). *The psychologically battered child.* San Francisco: Jossey-Bass.

Geller, J. A. (1982). Conjoint therapy: Staff training and treatment of the abuser and the abused. In M. Roy (Ed.), *The abusive partner* (pp. 198-215). New York: Van Nostrand Reinhold.

Geller, J. A., & Walsh, J. (1977-1978). A treatment model for the abused spouse. *Victimology, 1,* 627-632.

Gelles, R. J., & Harrop, J. W. (1989). Violence, battering, and psychological distress among women. *Journal of Interpersonal Violence, 4,* 400-420.

Gillespie, D. L. (1971). Who has the power? The marital struggle. *Journal of Marriage and the Family, 33,* 445-458.

Girdano, D. A., & Everly, G. S. (1986). *Controlling stress and tension: A holistic approach.* Englewood Cliffs, NJ: Prentice-Hall.

Gondolf, E. W. (1985). Anger and oppression in men who batter: Empiricist and feminist perspectives and their implications for research. *Victimology: An International Journal, 10,* 311-324.

Gondolf, E. W. (1988). The effect of batterer counseling on shelter outcome. *Violence and Victims, 3*(3), 275-289.

Goodwin, J. (1985). Family violence: Principles of intervention and prevention. *Hospital and Community Psychiatry, 36,* 1074-1079.

Goolkasian, G. A. (1986). *Confronting domestic violence: A guide for criminal justice agencies.* Washington, DC: National Institute of Justice.

Gordon, L. (1988). *Heroes of their own lives: The politics and history of family violence—Boston 1880-1960.* New York: Viking Penguin.

Gordon, M. (1964). *Assimilation in American life.* New York: Oxford University Press.

Gottfredson, S. D., & Gottfredson, D. M. (1988). Violence prediction methods: Statistical and clinical strategies. *Violence and Victims, 3,* 303-324.

Gottman, J., Notarius, C., Gonso, J., & Markman, H. (1976). *A couple's guide to communication.* Champaign, IL: Research Press.

Graham, D. L. R., Rawlings, E., & Rimini, N. (1988). Survivors of terror. In K. Yllo & M. Bograd (Eds.), *Feminist perspectives on wife abuse* (pp. 217-233). Newbury Park, CA: Sage.

Grusznski, R. J., & Carrillo, T. P. (1988). Who completes batterers' treatment group? An empirical investigation. *Journal of Family Violence, 3,* 141-150.

Halpern, M. (1984, August). *Battered women's alternatives: The men's program component.* Paper presented at the meeting of the American Psychological Association, Toronto.

Halsey, P. (1987). What can the church do? In M. Pellauer, B. Chester, & J. Boyajian (Eds.), *Sexual assault and abuse: A handbook for clergy and religious professionals* (pp. 219-222). New York: Harper & Row.

Hamberger, L. K., & Hastings, J. E. (1986). Personality correlates of men who abuse their partners: A cross-validation study. *Violence and Victims, 1*(4), 323-341.

Hamberger, L. K., & Hastings, J. E. (1988). Skill training for treatment of spouse abusers: An outcome study. *Journal of Family Violence, 3,* 121-130.

Hamberger, L. K., & Hastings, J. E. (1990). Recidivism following spouse abatement counseling: Treatment program implications. *Violence and Victims, 5*(3), 157-170.

Hamberger, L. K., Hastings, J. E., & Lohr, J. M. (1988, November). Cognitive and personality correlates of men who batter: Some continuities and discontinuities. Presented in A. Holtzworth-Monroe (Chair), *Research on marital violence: What we know, how we can apply it,* a symposium presented at the meeting of the Association for the Advancement of Behavior Therapy, New York.

Hamberger, L. K., & Lohr, J. M. (1989). Proximal causes of spouse abuse: A theoretical analysis for cognitive-behavioral interventions. In P. L. Caesar & L. K. Hamberger (Eds.), *Treatment of men who batter* (pp. 53-76). New York: Springer.

Hanneke, C. R., Shields, N. M., & McCall, G. J. (1986). Assessing the prevalence of marital rape. *Journal of Interpersonal Violence, 1,* 350-362.

Harris, J. (1986). Counseling violent couples using Walker's model. *Psychotherapy, 23,* 613-621.

Hart, B. (1988). *Safety for women: Monitoring batterers' programs.* Harrisburg: Pennsylvania Coalition Against Domestic Violence.

Hastings, J. E., & Hamberger, L. K. (1988). Personality characteristics of spouse abusers: A controlled comparison. *Violence and Victims, 3*(1), 31-48.

Hathaway, S. R., & Meehl, P. E. (1951). *An atlas for the clinical use of the MMPI.* Minneapolis: University of Minnesota Press.

Hawkins, R., & Beauvais, C. (1985, August). *Evaluation of group therapy with abusive men: The police record.* Paper presented at the meeting of the American Psychological Association, Los Angeles.

Henderson, S., Duncan-Jones, P., Byrne, D. G., & Scott, R. (1980). Measuring social relationships: The Interview Schedule for Social Interaction. *Psychological Medicine, 10,* 723-734.

Henderson, S., Duncan-Jones, P. Byrne, D. G., Scott, R., & Adcock, S. (1979). Psychiatric disorder in Canberra: A standardised study of prevalence. *Acta Psychiatrica Scandinavica, 60,* 355-374.

Hirschel, J. D., Hutchison, I. W., III, & Dean, C. W. (1992). The failure of arrest to deter spouse abuse. *Journal of Research in Crime and Delinquency, 29,* 7-33.

Homant, R. J. (1985). The police and spouse abuse: A review of recent findings. *Police Studies, 8,* 163-172.

Hotaling, G. T., & Sugarman, D. B. (1986). An analysis of risk markers in husband to wife violence: The current state of knowledge. *Violence and Victims, 1*(2), 101-124.

Hudson, W. W., & McIntosh, S. R. (1981). The assessment of spouse abuse: Two quantifiable dimensions. *Journal of Marriage and the Family, 43*, 873-885.

Hunt, D. M. (1990). Spouse abuse: Care goes beyond the office door. *Postgraduate Medicine, 87*(2), 130-135.

Jacobson, N. S., & Holtzworth-Munroe, A. (1986). Marital therapy: A social learning-cognitive perspective. In N. S. Jacobson & A. S. Gurman (Eds.), *Clinical handkbook of marital therapy* (pp. 29-70). New York: Guilford.

Jacobson, N. S., & Margolin, G. (1979). *Marital therapy: Strategies based on social learning and behavioral exchange principles.* New York: Brunner/Mazel.

Jaffe, P. G., Wolfe, D. A., & Wilson, S. K. (1990). *Children of battered women.* Newbury Park, CA: Sage.

Jennings, J. L. (1987). History and issues in the treatment of battering men: A case for unstructured group therapy. *Journal of Family Violence, 2*, 193-214.

Jones, L. E. (1991). The Minnesota School Curriculum Project: A statewide domestic violence prevention project in secondary schools. In B. Levy (Ed.), *Dating violence: Young women in danger* (pp. 258-266). Seattle, WA: Seal.

Jouriles, E. N., & O'Leary, K. D. (1985). Interspousal reliability of reports of marital violence. *Journal of Consulting and Clinical Psychology, 53*, 419-421.

Kappel, S., & Leuteritz, E. (1980). Wife battering in the Federal Republic of Germany. *Victimology, 5*, 225-239.

Klingbeil, K. S. (1986). Interpersonal violence: A hospital based model from policy to program. *Response, 9*, 6-9.

Koss, M. P., Gidycz, C. A., & Wisniewski, N. (1987). The scope of rape: Incidence and prevalence of sexual aggression and victimization in a national sample of higher education students. *Journal of Consulting and Clinical Psychology, 55*, 162-170.

Kuhn, T. S. (1962). *The structure of scientific revolutions.* Chicago: University of Chicago Press.

Kumagai, F. (1979). Social class, power and husband-wife violence in Japan. *Journal of Comparative Family Studies, 10*, 91-105.

Kumagai, F. (1981). Field theory and conjugal violence in Japan. *Journal of Comparative Family Studies, 12*, 413-428.

Kunkel, J. H. (1975). *Behavior, social problems, and change.* Englewood Cliffs, NJ: Prentice-Hall.

Kurz, D. (1987). Emergency department responses to battered women: Resistance to medicalization. *Social Problems, 34*, 69-81.

Lane, G., & Russell, T. (1989). Second-order systemic work with violent couples. In P. L. Caesar & L. K. Hamberger (Eds.), *Treatment men who batter* (pp. 134-162). New York: Springer.

LaViolette, A. D., Barnett, O. W., & Miller, C. L. (1984, August). *A classification of wife abusers on the Bem sex-role inventory.* Paper presented at the Second Annual Conference on Research and Domestic Violence.

Leong, D. J., Coates, C. J., & Hoskins, J. (1987). *Follow-up of batterers treated in a court-ordered treatment program.* Paper presented at the Third National Family Violence Research Conference, University of New Hampshire, Durham.

Lerman, L. G. (1986). Prosecution of wife beaters: Institutional obstacles and innovations. In M. Lystad (Ed.), *Violence in the home.* New York: Brunner/Mazel.

Levy, B. (1984). *Skills for violence free relationships.* Santa Monica: Southern California Coalition for Battered Women.

Levy, B. (Ed.). (1991). *Dating violence: Young women in danger.* Seattle, WA: Seal.

Libow, J. A., Raskin, P. A., & Caust, B. L. (1982). Feminist and family systems therapy: Are they irreconcilable? *American Journal of Family Therapy, 10,* 3-12.

Lindquist, C. U., Telch, C. F., & Taylor, J. (1985). Evaluation of a conjugal violence treatment program: A pilot study. *Behavioral Counseling and Community Intervention, 3,* 76-90.

Lum, D. (1986). *Social work practice and people of color.* Monterey, CA: Brooks/Cole.

MacEwen, K. E., & Barling, J. (1988). Multiple stressors, violence in the family of origin, and marital aggression: A longitudinal investigation. *Journal of Family Violence, 3*(1), 73-88.

Mahoney, M. J. (1976). *Scientist as subjects: The psychological imperative.* Cambridge, MA: Ballinger.

Maiden, P., & Tolman, R. M. (1989). *Assessment of family violence in EAP settings.* Paper presented at the National Association of Social Work, San Francisco.

Maiuro, R. D., Cahn, T. S., & Vitaliano, P. P. (1986). Assertiveness deficits and hostility in domestically violent men. *Violence and Victims, 1*(4), 279-289.

Maiuro, R. D., Cahn, T. S., Vitaliano, P. P., Wagner, B. C., & Zegree, J. B. (1988). Anger, hostility, and depression in domestically violent versus generally assaultive men and nonviolent control subjects. *Journal of Consulting and Clinical Psychology, 56*(1), 17-23.

Maiuro, R. D., & Wood, L. (1988, April). *An eclectic-multimodal approach to treatment of domestic violence.* Paper presented at the meeting of the Western Psychological Association, San Francisco.

Margolin, G. (1979). Conjoint marital therapy to enhance anger management and reduce spouse abuse. *American Journal of Family Therapy, 7,* 13-24.

Margolin, G., John, R., & Gleberman, L. (1988). Affective responses to conflictual discussions in violent and nonviolent couples. *Journal of Consulting and Clinical Psychology, 56*(1), 24-33.

McDonald, G. W. (1980). Family power: The assessment of a decade of theory and research, 1970-1979. *Journal of Marriage and the Family, 42,* 841-854.

McDowell, N. (1990). Person, assertion, and marriage: On the nature of household violence in Bun. *Pacific Studies, 13,* 171-188.

McKay, M., Rogers, P. D., & McKay, J. (1989). *When anger lasts: Quieting the storm within.* Oakland, CA: New Harbinger.

McLeer, S. V. (1988). Psychoanalytic perspectives on family violence. In V. B. Van Hasselt, R. L. Morrison, A. S. Bellack, & M. Hersen (Eds.), *Handbook of family violence* (pp. 11-30). New York: Plenum.

McLeer, S. V., & Anwar, R. (1989). A study of battered women presenting in an emergency department. *American Journal of Public Health, 79,* 65-66.

Meichenbaum, D. (1977). *Cognitive-behavior modification.* New York: Plenum.

Mercy, J. A., & Saltzman, L. E. (1989). Fatal violence among spouses in the United States, 1976-1985. *American Journal of Public Health, 79,* 595-599.

Miller, J. L., & Whittaker, J. K. (1988). Social services and social support: Blended programs for families at risk of child maltreatment. *Child Welfare, 67,* 161-174.

Millon, T. (1983). *Millon Clinical Multiaxial Inventory.* Minneapolis: National Computer Systems.

Mitchell, R. E., & Hodson, C. A. (1983). Coping with domestic violence: Social support and psychological health among battered women. *American Journal of Community Psychology, 11*(6), 629-654.

Mitchell, W. E. (1990). Why Wape men don't beat their wives: Constraints toward domestic tranquility in a New Guinea society. *Pacific Studies, 13,* 141-150.

Monahan, J. (1981). *Predicting violent behavior: An assessment of clinical techniques.* Beverly Hills, CA: Sage.

National Crime Surveys. (1981). *National Crime Surveys: National sample. 1973-1979.* Ann Arbor, MI: Inter-University Consortium Political and Social Research.

Neidig, P. H. (1984). Women's shelters, men's collectives and other issues in the field of spouse abuse. *Victimology, 9,* 464-476.

Neidig, P. H., & Friedman, D. H. (1984). *Spouse abuse: A treatment program for couples.* Champaign, IL: Research Press.

Neidig, P. H., Friedman, D. H., & Collins, B. S. (1985). Domestic conflict containment: A spouse abuse treatment program. *Social Casework, 66,* 195-204.

Nelson, K. E., Landsman, M. J., & Deutelbaum, W. (1990). Three models of family-centered placement prevention services. *Child Welfare, 69,* 3-21.

Nietzel, M. T., Winett, R. A., MacDonald, M. L., & Davidson, W. S. (1977). *Behavioral approaches to community psychology.* New York: Pergamon.

Novaco, R. W. (1975). *Anger control: The development and evaluation of an experimental treatment.* Lexington, MA: D. C. Heath.

O'Leary, K. D., & Curley, A. D. (1986). Assertion and family violence: Correlates of spouse abuse. *Journal of Marital and Family Therapy, 12,* 281-289.

Pagelow, M. D. (1981). *Woman-battering.* Beverly Hills, CA: Sage.

Parker, J. C., & Saunders, D. G. (1989). *Socio-demographic factors and treatment follow-through in groups for men who batter.* Manuscript submitted for publication.

Patterson, G. R., & Hops, H. (1972). Coercion, a game for two: Intervention techniques for marital conflict. In R. E. Ulrich & P. T. Mountjoy (Eds.), *The experimental analysis of social behavior* (pp. 424-440). New York: Appleton-Century-Crofts.

Pellauer, M. (1983). Violence against women: The theological dimension. *Christianity and Crisis, 43,* 206-212.

Peltoniemi, T. (1982). Current research on family violence in Finland and Sweden. *Victimology, 7,* 252-255.

Pence, E. (1983). The Duluth Domestic Abuse Intervention Project. *Hamline Law Review, 6,* 247-275.

Pence, E. (1989). Batterer programs: Shifting from community collusion to community confrontation. In P. L. Caesar & L. K. Hamberger (Eds.), *Treatment men who batter* (pp. 24-50). New York: Springer.

Pence, E., Novack, S., & Galaway, B. (1982). *Domestic Abuse Intervention Project: Six month research report.* Unpublished manuscript from the Duluth (Minnesota) Domestic Abuse Intervention Project.

Pence, E., & Shepard, M. (1988). Integrating feminist theory and practice. In K. Yllo & M. Bograd (Eds.), *Feminist perspectives on wife abuse* (pp. 282-298). Newbury Park, CA: Sage.

Pinderhughes, E. (1989). *Understanding race, ethnicity and power.* New York: Free Press.

Pirog-Good, M., & Stets-Kealey, J. (1985). Male batterers and battering prevention programs: A national survey. *Response, 8,* 8-12.

Pleck, E. H. (1987). *Domestic tyranny: The making of social policy against family violence from colonial times to present.* New York: Oxford University Press.

Pokorny, A. D., Miller, B. A., & Kaplan, H. B. (1972). The brief MAST: A shortened version of the Michigan Alcoholism Screening Test. *American Journal of Psychiatry, 129(3)*, 342-345.

Purdy, F., & Nickle, N. (1981). Practice principles for working with groups of men who batter. *Social Work with Groups, 4*, 111-122.

Quinsey, V. L., & Maguire, A. (1986). Maximum security psychiatric patients: Actuarial and clinical prediction of dangerousness. *Journal of Interpersonal Violence, 1*, 143-172.

Rabin, C., Sens, M., & Rosenthal, H. (1982). Home-based marital therapy for multiproblem families. *Journal of Marital and Family Therapy, 8*, 451-461.

Rauma, D. (1984). Going for the gold: Prosecutorial decision making in cases of wife assault. *Social Science Research, 13*, 321-351.

Riding, A. (1985, September 14). Brazil's abused women find refuge in precinct. *New York Times*, p. 4.

Rollins, B. C., & Bahr, S. J. (1976). A theory of power relationship in marriage. *Journal of Marriage and the Family, 38*, 619-627.

Rooney, R. H. (1988). Socialization strategies for involuntary clients. *Social Casework, 69*, 131-140.

Rose, S. D. (1989). *Working with adults in groups.* San Francisco: Jossey-Bass.

Rosenbaum, A. (1986). Of men, macho, and marital violence. *Journal of Family Violence, 1(2)*, 121-130.

Rosenbaum, A. (1988). Methodological issues in marital violence research. *Journal of Family Violence, 3(2)*, 91-104.

Rosenbaum, A., & Maiuro, R. D. (1989). Eclectic approaches in working with men who batter. In P. L. Caesar & L. K. Hamberger (Eds.), *Treating men who batter: Theory, practice and programs* (pp. 165-195). New York: Springer.

Rosenbaum, A., & O'Leary, K. D. (1981a). Children: the unintended victims of marital violence. *American Journal of Orthopsychiatry, 51*, 692-699.

Rosenbaum, A., & O'Leary, K. D. (1981b). Marital violence: Characteristics of abusive couples. *Journal of Consulting & Clinical Psychology, 49(1)*, 63-71.

Rosenbaum, A., & O'Leary, K. D. (1986). The treatment of marital violence. In N. S. Jacobson & A. S. Gurman (Eds.), *Clinical handbook of marital therapy* (pp. 385-405). New York: Guilford.

Rosenbaum, M., & Bennett, B. (1988). Homicide and depression. *American Journal of Psychiatry, 143*, 367-370.

Roy, M. (1977). A current survey of 150 cases. In *Battered women: A psychosociological study of domestic violence.* New York: Van Nostrand Reinhold.

Russell, D. E. (1982). *Rape in marriage.* New York: Macmillan.

Safilios-Rothschild, C. (1970). The study of family power structure: A review 1960-1969. *Journal of Marriage and the Family, 32*, 539-552.

Saunders, D. G. (1982). Counseling the violent husband. In P. A. Keller & L. G. Ritt (Eds.), *Innovations in clinical practice* (Vol. 1, pp. 16-29). Sarasota, FL: Professional Resource Exchange.

Saunders, D. G. (1989). Cognitive-behavioral interventions with men who batter: Applications and outcome. In P. L. Caesar & L. K. Hamberger (Eds.), *Treatment of men who batter* (pp. 77-100). New York: Springer.

Saunders, D. G. (1992). Women battering. In R. T. Ammerman and M. Hersen (Eds.), *Assessment of family violence: A clinical and legal sourcebook* (pp. 208-235). New York: Wiley.

Saunders, D. G., & Hanusa, D. (1986). Cognitive-behavioral treatment of men who batter: The short-term effects of group therapy. *Journal of Family Violence, 1*(4), 357-372.

Saunders, D. G., & Parker, J. (1989). *Legal sanctions and treatment follow-through among men who batter: A multivariate analysis.* Manuscript submitted for publication.

Scaglion, R. (1990). Spare the rod and spoil the woman? Family violence in Abelam society. *Pacific Studies, 13,* 189-204.

Schechter, S. (1982). *Women and male violence: The visions and struggles of the battered women's movement.* Boston: South End.

Shepard, M. (1987, July). *Intervention with men who batter: An evaluation of a domestic abuse program.* Paper presented at the Third National Family Violence Conference for Researchers, Durham, New Hampshire.

Sherman, L. W., & Berk, R. A. (1984). The specific deterrent effects of arrest for domestic assault. *American Sociological Review, 49,* 261-272.

Sherman, L. W., Schmidt, J. D., Rogan, D. P., Gartin, P. R., Cohn, E. G., Collins, D. J., & Bacich, A. R. (1991). From initial deterence to long-term escalation: Short-custody arrest for poverty ghetto domestic violence. *Criminology, 29,* 821-849.

Shields, N. M., McCall, G. J., & Hanneke, C. R. (1988). Patterns of family and nonfamily violence: Violent husbands and violent men. *Violence and Victims, 3*(2), 83-97.

Shipley, W. C. (1940). A self-administering scale for measuring intellectual impairment and deterioration. *Journal of Psychology, 9,* 371-377.

Singh, G. (1986). Violence against wives in India. *Response, 9,* 16-18.

Skinner, B. F. (1974). *About behaviorism.* New York: Knopf.

Soler, E. (1987). Domestic violence is a crime: A case study—San Francisco Family Violence Project. In D. J. Sonkin (Ed.), *Domestic violence on trial* (pp. 21-35). New York: Springer.

Soler, E., & Martin, S. (1983). *Domestic violence is a crime.* San Francisco: Family Violence Project.

Sonkin, D. (1988). The male batterer: Clinical and research issues. *Violence and Victims, 3*(1), 65-79.

Sonkin, D. J., & Durphy, M. (1985). *Learning to live without violence.* San Francisco: Volcano Press.

Spitzer, J. R. (1985). *Spousal abuse in rabbinic and contemporary Judaism.* New York: National Federation of Temple Sisterhoods.

Starr, R. H., Jr. (1988). Physical abuse of children. In V. B. Van Hasselt, R. L. Morrision, A. S. Bellack, & M. Hersen (Eds.), *Handbook of family violence* (pp. 119-155). New York: Plenum.

Steinman, M. (1988). Evaluating a system-wide response to domestic violence: Some initial findings. *Journal of Contemporary Criminal Justice, 4,* 172-186.

Steinman, M. (1990). Lowering recidivism among men who batter women. *Journal of Police Science and Administration, 17,* 124-132.

Stordeur, R. A., & Stille, R. (1989). *Ending men's violence against their partners: One road to peace.* Newbury Park, CA: Sage.

Straus, M. A. (1979). Measuring intrafamilial conflict and violence: The conflict tactics (CT) scale. *Journal of Marriage and the Family, 45,* 75-78.

Straus, M. A. (1980). Social stress and marital violence in a national sample of American families. In F. Wright, C. Bahn, & R. Reiber (Eds.), *Forensic psychology and psychiatry.* New York: New York Academy of Sciences.

Straus, M. A. (1986). Medical care costs of intrafamily assault and homicide. *Bulletin of the New York Academy of Medicine, 62,* 556-561.

Straus, M. A., & Gelles, R. J. (1986). Societal change and change in family violence from 1975 to 1985 as revealed by two national surveys. *Journal of Marriage and the Family, 48,* 465-479.

Straus, M. A., & Gelles, R. J. (1987). The costs of family violence. *Public Health Reports, 102,* 638-641.

Straus, M. A., & Gelles, R. J. (1988). How violent are American families? Estimates from the National Family Violence Resurvey and other studies. In G. T. Hotaling, D. Finkelhor, J. T. Kirkpatrick, & M. A. Straus (Eds.), *Family abuse and its consequences* (pp. 14-36). Newbury Park, CA: Sage.

Straus, M. A., & Gelles, R. J. (Eds.). (1990). *Physical violence in American families.* New Brunswick, NJ: Transaction.

Straus, M. A., Gelles, R. J., & Steinmetz, S. K. (1980). *Behind closed doors.* Garden City, NY: Anchor/Doubleday.

Straus, M. A., Sweet, S., & Vissing, Y. M. (1989). *Verbal aggression against spouses and children in a nationally representative sample of American families.* Paper presented at the annual meeting of the Speech Communication Association, San Francisco, CA.

Stuart, R. B. (1980). *Helping couples change.* New York: Guilford.

Sullivan, C. M. (1991). The provision of advocacy services to women leaving abusive partners: An exploratory study. *Journal of Interpersonal Violence, 6,* 41-54.

Sullivan, G. (1982). Cooptation of alternative services: The Battered Women's Movement as a case study. *Catalyst, 14,* 39-56.

Syers, M., & Edleson, J. L. (in press). The combined effects of coordinated criminal justice intervention in woman abuse. *Journal of Interpersonal Violence.*

Syers-McNairy, M. (1990). *Women who leave violent relationships: Getting on with life.* Unpublished doctoral dissertation, University of Minnesota, Minneapolis.

Szinovacz, M. E. (1983). Using couple data as a methodological tool: The case of marital violence. *Journal of Marriage and the Family, 45,* 633-644.

Taylor, J. W. (1984). Structured conjoint therapy for spouse abuse cases. *Social Casework, 65,* 11-18.

Thurman v. City of Torrington, 595 F. Supp. 1521 (D. Conn. 1984).

Tolman, R. M. (1988). The initial development of a measure of psychological maltreatment of women by their male partners. *Violence and Victims, 4,* 159-178.

Tolman, R. M. (1990, September). *The impact of group process on outcome of groups for men who batter.* Paper presented at the European Congress on the Advancement of Behavior Therapy, Paris.

Tolman, R. M. (1991). *Validation of the psychological maltreatment of women inventory: Preliminary report.* Unpublished paper, University of Illinois at Chicago.

Tolman, R. M. (in press). Psychological abuse of women. In R. Ammerman & M. Hersen (Eds.), *Assessment of family violence: A clinical and legal sourcebook.* New York: John Wiley.

Tolman, R. M., Beeman, S., & Mendoza, C. (1987, July). *The effectiveness of a shelter-sponsored program for men who batter.* Paper presented at the Third National Family Violence Research Conference, Durham, NH.

Tolman, R. M., & Bennett, L. W. (1990). A review of quantitative research on men who batter. *Journal of Interpersonal Violence, 5,* 87-118.

Tolman, R. M., & Bhosley, G. (1989). A comparison of two types of pregroup preparation for men who batter. *Journal of Social Service Research, 13,* 33-44.

Tolman, R. M., & Bhosley, G. (1991). The outcome of participation in shelter-sponsored program for men who batter. In D. Knudsen & J. Miller (Eds.), *Abused and battered: Social and legal responses to family violence* (pp. 113-122). Hawthorne, NY: Aldine de Gruyter.

Tolman, R. M., & Edleson, J. L. (1989). Cognitive-behavioral intervention with men who batter. In B. A. Thyer (Ed.), *Behavioral family therapy* (pp. 169-190). Springfield, IL: Charles C Thomas.

Tolman, R. M., & Saunders, D. G. (1988). The case for the cautious use of anger control with men who batter. *Response, 11,* 15-20.

Truesdell, D. L., McNeil, J. S., & Deschner, J. P. (1986). Incidence of wife abuse in incestuous families. *Social Work, 31,* 138-140.

United Nations. (1979). *Convention on the elimination of all forms of discrimination against women.* New York: Author.

United Nations. (1987). *Report of the expert group meeting on violence in the family with special emphasis on its effects on women.* Vienna, Austria: U.N. Branch for the Advancement of Women.

Videka-Sherman, L. (1988). Metaanalysis of research on social work practice in mental health. *Social Work, 33,* 325-337.

Waldo, M. (1986). Group counseling for military personnel who battered their wives. *Journal for Specialists in Group Work, 11,* 132-138.

Walker, L. E. (1979). *The battered woman.* New York: Harper & Row.

Wolfe, D. A., Wolfe, V., & Best, C. L. (1988). Child victims of sexual abuse. In V. B. Van Hasselt, R. L. Morrision, A. S. Bellack, & M. Hersen (Eds.), *Handbook of family violence* (pp. 157-185). New York: Plenum.

Women's Crisis Centre. (1990). *Becoming whole: A handbook for working with abused women.* Penang, Malaysia: Author.

Woolfolk, R. L., & Lehrer, P. M. (1984). *Principles and practice of stress management.* New York: Guilford.

Index

About the Authors

Jeffrey L. Edleson is a social worker with extensive experience in conducting groups for both adults and children. He has published numerous articles and several books on topics that include domestic violence, group work, and program evaluation. He is Professor in the School of Social Work at the University of Minnesota. He has conducted research at the Domestic Abuse Project in Minneapolis for almost 10 years and is its Director of Evaluation and Research. He also conducts research and provides technical assistance to domestic violence programs in Israel and Singapore. His books include *Working with Children and Adolescents in Groups* (coauthored with Sheldon Rose; 1987). He is on the editorial boards of the *Journal of Interpersonal Violence, Violence Update,* and *Research on Social Work Practice.* He graduated Phi Beta Kappa from the University of California at Berkeley and completed master's and doctoral degrees at the University of Wisconsin at Madison.

Richard M. Tolman (Ph.D.) is currently an Associate Professor at the Jane Addams College of Social Work, University of Illinois at Chicago. He received his undergraduate degree from Northwestern University and his M.S.W. from the University of Michigan, Ann Arbor. He is a consultant and practitioner at the Sarah's Inn Program for Men in Oak Park, Illinois, a program for men who batter. Dr. Tolman began his work with men who batter in Anchorage, Alaska, in 1980, and has remained involved in direct practice and research on abuse against women since that time. He is an Associate Editor of the *Journal of Interpersonal Violence* and a member of the board of governors of *Violence Update*.

Interpersonal Violence:
The Practice Series

Series Editor: **JON R. CONTE**, The University of Washington

SAGE PUBLICATIONS, INC.
P.O. BOX 5084
THOUSAND OAKS, CALIFORNIA 91359-9924

Place
Stamp
here